Susie Rankin

EYE-WITNESSES TO WAGON TRAINS WEST

Eye-Witnesses to Wagon Trains West

Edited by James Hewitt

Charles Scribner's Sons
New York

Printed in Great Britain
Library of Congress Catalog Card Number 74-465
ISBN 0-684-13864-6

Preface

Eye-Witnesses to Wagon Trains West recreates, through the recorded experiences of men, women, and children who took part, some significant journeys by wagon train across the American continent from east to west during the eighteen-forties. When families set out from the eastern states to settle in California, Oregon, and Utah, they were continuing a westward movement that had begun when the Atlantic seaboard had been settled two centuries before. But there was this remarkable feature: whereas it had taken two hundred years for the frontier to be pushed a thousand miles, to the edge of the great but forbidding plains west of the Mississippi River, the next stage was not to be the logical continuation, to the plains themselves, but an awe-inspiring leap of twice that distance to the Pacific seaboard.

In the early eighteen-forties Oregon and California were extolled by some journalists, authors, lecturers, and politicians as being the nearest thing possible to Paradise on earth. They had an ideal climate, were well watered and timbered, had rich soil and lush pasturage. Further, it only required a few thousand Americans to settle in these territories for them to become American states. Oregon was already claimed by America, in dispute with Great Britain. California was controlled by Mexico, but with a weak and shaky hold. After all, Texas had once been Mexican, but was now American.

The Mormon exodus to uninhabited Salt Lake Valley was the result of persecution and of a deep desire to find an isolated place where the community and their faith could grow in peace.

Each of the five sections of this book reconstructs an overland

v

crossing from eye-witness accounts: the first real emigrant caravan organized by young schoolteacher John Bidwell in 1841; the 'great emigration' to Oregon in '43, when the determination of Dr Marcus Whitman took wagons for the first time through to the Columbia River and down it; the disaster which befell the Donner party, when during the migration of '46 to California they were caught in snow blizzards in the Sierras, and the survivors among them were driven to eating the flesh of their dead comrades; the Mormon trek in '47 to make the desert bloom; and finally the crazed rush to the Californian gold diggings in '49.

There were no roads to follow, merely faintly marked trails blazed by fur-trappers, traders, government explorers, and missionaries to the Indians. The method of family transportation was the covered wagon, drawn by mules or oxen, mostly three yoke of the latter; and in pushing across treeless plains, alkali deserts, and formidable mountain ranges, emigrants had to contend with excessive heat and cold, thirst and hunger, dysentery and cholera.

The eye-witness accounts used in this book come from a variety of sources: memoirs, diaries, journals, letters, reports, and published interviews. Most helpful for narrative flow were works written up from journals; trail diaries themselves are often of staccato brevity. With emigrants coming from all levels of society, inevitably the sophistication and style of the writing varies widely. But all extracts are presented in this book as they were originally written—thus retaining their immediacy—even where there are marked eccentricities of style, spelling, grammar, or punctuation.

JAMES HEWITT

Contents

Acknowledgements

Thanks are due to Arthur G. Arnott and the United States Information Service Press Office in London for supplying plates 7 and 22, and to the Trustees of the British Museum for supplying the rest of the photographs. All the maps except that on page xi are redrawn from Archer B. Hulbert's *Forty-Niners* (Boston, 1931).

Illustrations

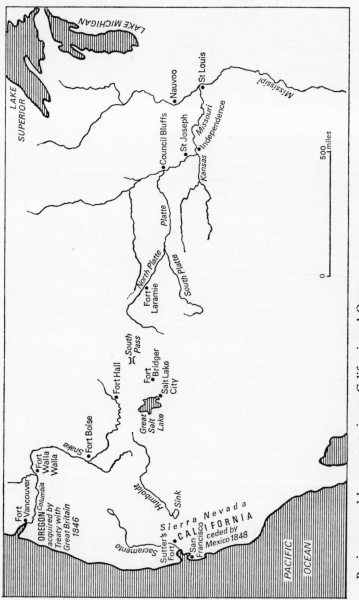

1. Region crossed by wagon trains to California and Oregon

The Advance Guard:
The Bidwell/Bartleson Party,
1841

The first true emigrant party to cross the continent to California was that organized by John Bidwell, a young schoolteacher, in 1841. In his written account of the journey, he claimed: 'The party whose fortunes I have followed across the plains was not only the first that went direct to California from the east, we were probably the first white people, except Bonneville's Party of 1833, that ever crossed the Sierra Nevada.' In fact, the Sierra had been crossed in the spring of 1827 by Jedediah Smith, Robert Evans, and Silas Gobel. And other 'mountain men' (as the fur-trappers were called) had been in and out of California for many years before Bidwell's party made the crossing. But Bidwell could claim to have taken the first real emigrant party, which included a woman and a child, and that alone justifies their place among the pioneers of western settlement. In his History of California *(San Francisco, 1885) the historian T. H. Hiltell called them 'the advance guard of the irresistible march of the American people westward'.*

John Bidwell was born of English parents in Chautauqua County, New York, on 5 August 1819. A sequence of family moves terminated in Ohio, whence, at the age of twenty, Bidwell set out to test life in frontier Missouri. This is his description of the region which acted as a springboard for overland crossings to the Pacific west throughout the eighteen-forties:

The Platte Purchase, as it was called, had been recently bought from the Indians, and was newly but thickly settled, on account of its proximity to navigation, its fine timber, good water and unsurpassed fertility.

On the route I traveled I cannot recall seeing an emigrant wagon in Missouri. The western movement which subsequently filled Missouri and other western states and overflowed into the adjoining territories, had then hardly begun, except as to Platte County. The contest in Congress over the Platte Purchase, which by increasing the area of Missouri gave more territory to slavery, called wide attention to that charming region. The anti-slavery sentiment even at that date ran quite high. This was, I believe, the first addition to slave territory after the Missouri Compromise. But slavery won. The rush that followed in the space of one or two years filled the most desirable part of the Purchase to overflowing. The imagination could not conceive a finer country—lovely, rolling, and fertile, wonderfully productive, beautifully arranged for settlement, part prairie and part timber. The land was unsurveyed. Every settler had aimed to locate half a mile from his neighbor, and there was as yet no conflict. Peace and contentment reigned. Nearly every place seemed to have a beautiful spring of clear cold water. The hills and prairies and the level places were alike covered with a black and fertile soil. I cannot recall seeing an acre of poor ground in Platte County. Of course there was intense longing on the part of the people of Missouri to have the Indians removed and a corresponding desire, as soon as the purchase was consummated, to get possession of the beautiful land. It was in some sense, perhaps, a kind of Oklahoma movement. Another feature was the abundance of wild honey-bees. Every tree that had a hollow in it seemed to be a bee tree, and every hollow was full of rich, golden honey. A singular fact which I learned from old hunters was that the honey-bee was never found more than seventy or eighty miles in advance of the white settlements on the frontier. On this attractive land I set my affections, intending to make it my home.

On my arrival, my money being all spent, I was obliged to accept the first thing that offered, and I began teaching school in the country about five miles from the town of Weston, which was located on the north side of the Missouri River and about four miles above Fort Leavenworth in Kansas Territory. Possibly some may suppose it did not take much education to teach a country school at that period in Missouri. The rapid settlement of that new region had brought together people of all classes and conditions, and had thrown into juxtaposition almost every phase of intelligence as well as illiteracy. But there was no lack of self-reliance or native shrewdness in any class, and I must say I learned to have a high esteem for the people, among whom I found warm and lifelong friends.

But even in Missouri there were drawbacks. Rattlesnakes and copperheads were abundant. One man, it was said, found a place to suit him, but on alighting from his horse so many snakes greeted him that he decided to go farther. At his second attempt, finding more snakes instead of fewer, he left the country altogether. I taught school there in all about a year. My arrival was in June, 1839, and in the fall of that year the surveyors came on to lay out the country; the lines ran every way, sometimes through a man's house, sometimes through his barn, so that there was much confusion and trouble about boundaries, etc. By the favor of certain men, and by paying a small amount for a little piece of fence here and a small clearing there, I got a claim, and proposed to make it my home, and have my father remove there from Ohio.

In the following summer, 1840, the weather was very hot, so that during the vacation I could do but little work on my place, and needing some supplies—books, clothes, etc.—I concluded to take a trip to St. Louis, which I did by way of the Missouri River. The distance was 600 miles by water; the down trip occupied two days, and was one of the most delightful experiences of my life. But returning, the river being low and full of snags, and the steamboat heavily laden—the boats were generally lightly loaded going down—we were continually getting on sandbars, and were delayed nearly a month.

This trip proved to be the turning point in my life, for while I was gone a man had 'jumped' my land. Generally in such cases public sentiment was against the jumper, and it was decidedly so in my case. But the scoundrel held on. He was a bully—had killed a man in Callaway County—and everybody seemed afraid of him. Influential friends of mine tried to persuade him to let me have eighty acres, half of the claim. But he was stubborn, and said that all he wanted was just what the law allowed him. Unfortunately for me, he had the legal advantage. I had worked some now and then on the place, but had not actually lived on it. The law required a certain residence, and that the preëmptor should be twenty-one years of age or a man of family. I was neither, and could do nothing. Naturally all I had earned had been spent upon the land, and when it was taken I lost about everything I had. There being no possibility of getting another claim to suit me, I resolved to go elsewhere when spring should open.[5]

The 'elsewhere' the young schoolteacher's thoughts turned to was across 2,000 miles of plains, deserts, and mountains. His imagination was fired in that direction by reading a letter written by John Marsh, an American in California, and published in a St. Louis newspaper in the autumn of 1840, and by talking to a French trapper a few days later.

John Marsh was one of the small band of Americans then residing in California, where he combined ranching with doctoring. He had gone to California in 1836, at the age of thirty-six, presenting as a medical degree his Bachelor of Arts degree from Harvard, which, being in Latin, nobody in Southern California could read. Unable to pay the fees to become a doctor, he had nevertheless for a time worked as an assistant to a Boston physician, and later to an army surgeon at Fort St. Anthony. By charging twenty-five cows a professional call, he was able to build up a prosperous ranch. He seems to have made a reasonably good doctor : at any rate he was the only one there. He took into his home as 'house-keeper-wife' an Indian squaw.

Marsh considered—rightly, as it turned out—that if a few hundred Americans were to come into California they could soon make it part of the United States. Hence letters to friends in Missouri calling on them to come to California. One letter, which John Bidwell read with fascination, was published in the St. Louis Daily Argus. *Marsh had written :*

This is beyond all comparison the finest country and the finest climate. What we want here is more people. If we had fifty families from Missouri, we could do exactly as we please without any fear of being troubled.[28]

Though Marsh had himself entered Southern California—on horse-back, with his saddle-bags full of books on medicine and agriculture—by the Old Spanish Trail from Sante Fé, he advised :

The difficulty of coming here is imaginary. The route I would recommend is from Independence to the frontier rendezvous on Green River, then to Soda Spring on Bear River above the Big Salt Lake, thence to Mary's [*or Humboldt*] River until you come in sight of the gap in the great mountain, through that gap by a good road and you arrive in the plain of Joaquin, and down that river on a level plain through thousands of elk and horse. Three or four days journey and you come to my house.[28]

These few brief instructions were to act as 'guide-book' for the first emigrant party. A few days after reading Marsh's letter in the St. Louis newspaper, John Bidwell met and talked to a French fur-trapper called Antoine Roubidoux, whose words reinforced the impression of California made by those of Marsh. Many Missourians were now thinking of making the overland crossing.

Roubidoux described it as one of perennial spring and boundless fertility, and laid stress on the countless thousands of wild horses and cattle. . . . Every conceivable question that we could ask him was answered favorably. Generally the first question which a Missourian asked about a country was whether there was any fever and ague. I remember his answer distinctly. He said there was but one man in California that had ever had a chill there, and it was a matter of so much wonderment to the people of Monterey that they went eighteen miles into the country to see him shake. Nothing could have been more satisfactory on the score of health. He said that the Spanish authorities were most friendly, and that the people were the most hospitable on the globe; that you could travel all over California and it would cost you nothing for horses or feed. Even the Indians were friendly. His description of the country made it seem like a paradise.[5]

Bidwell had no difficulty in finding support for a caravan to make the overland crossing to California in the spring of '41.

We appointed a corresponding secretary and a committee to report a plan of organization. A pledge was drawn up in which every signer agreed to purchase a suitable outfit and to rendezvous at Sapling Grove in what is now the state of Kansas, on the ninth of the following May, armed and equipped to cross the Rocky Mountains to California. We called ourselves the Western Emigration Society, and as soon as the pledge was drawn up every one who agreed to come signed his name to it, and it took like wildfire. In a short time, I think within a month, we had about 500 names; we also had correspondence on the subject with people all over Missouri, and even as far east as Illinois and Kentucky, and as far south as Arkansas. As soon as the movement was announced in the papers we had many letters of inquiry and we expected people in considerable numbers to join us. About that time we heard of a man in Jackson County, Missouri, who had received a letter from a person in California named Dr. Marsh speaking favorably of the country, and a copy was published.

Our ignorance of the route was complete. We knew that California lay west, and that was the extent of our knowledge. Some of the maps consulted, supposed of course to be correct, showed a lake in the vicinity of where Salt Lake now is; it was represented as a long lake, three or four hundred miles in extent, narrow and with two outlets, both running into the Pacific Ocean, either apparently larger than the Mississippi River. . . . Even Frémont knew nothing about Salt Lake until 1843, when for the first time he explored it and mapped it correctly, his report being first printed, I believe, in 1845.

This being the first movement across the Rocky Mountains to California, it is not surprising that it suffered reverses before we were fairly started. One of these was the publication of a letter in a New York newspaper giving a depressing view of the country for which we were all so confidently longing. . . .

The result was that the people began to think more seriously about the scheme, the membership of the society began dropping off, and it so happened at last that of all the 500 that had signed the pledge I was the only one that got ready; and even I had hard work to do so, for I had barely means to buy a wagon, a gun, and provisions. Indeed, the man who was going with me and who was to furnish the horses, backed out and there I was with my wagon. . . .

At the last moment before the time to start for the rendezvous at Sapling Grove—it seemed almost providential—along came a man named George Henshaw, an invalid from Illinois, I think. He was pretty well dressed, was riding a fine black horse, and had ten or fifteen dollars. I persuaded him to let me take his horse and trade him for a yoke of steers to pull the wagon and a sorry-looking, one-eyed mule for him to ride. We went via Weston to lay in some supplies. One wagon and four or five persons here joined us. On

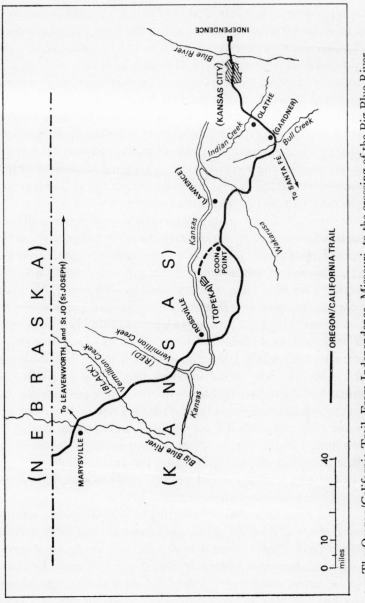

2. The Oregon/California Trail. From Independence, Missouri, to the crossing of the Big Blue River

leaving Weston, where there had been so much opposition, we were six or seven in number, and nearly half the town followed us for a mile, and some for five or six miles to bid us good-bye, . . . All expressed good wishes and desired to hear from us.

When we reached Sapling Grove . . . in May, 1841, there was but one wagon ahead of us. For the next few days one or two wagons would come each day, and among the recruits were three families from Arkansas. We organized by electing as captain of the company a man named Bartleson from Jackson County, Missouri. He was not the best man for the position, but we were given to understand that if he was not elected captain he would not go; and he had seven or eight men with him . . . Every one furnished his own supplies. The party consisted of sixty-nine, including men, women, and children. Our teams were of oxen, mules, and horses. We had no cows, as the later emigrants usually had, and the lack of milk was a great privation to the children. It was understood that every one should have not less than a barrel of flour, with sugar and so forth to suit, but I laid in one hundred pounds of flour more than the usual quantity, besides other things. This I did because we were told that when we got into the mountains we probably would get out of bread and have to live on meat alone, which I thought would kill me even if it did not others. My gun was an old flint-lock rifle, but a good one. Old hunters told me to have nothing to do with cap or percussion locks, that they were unreliable, and that if I got my caps or percussion wet I could not shoot, while if I lost my flint I could pick up another on the plains. I doubt whether there was one hundred dollars in the whole party, but all were enthusiastic and anxious to go.

In five days after my arrival we were ready to start, but no one knew where to go, not even the captain. . . .[5]

At this point the company had a stroke of good fortune, with the arrival of a small group of Catholic missionaries, led by a forty-years-old Belgian Jesuit, Father Pierre Jean de Smet, who at the age of twenty had gone to America to convert the Indians, and was now on his way to found a mission amongst the Flathead Indians of Oregon. The missionaries had with them as guide a celebrated mountain man in Thomas 'Broken Hand' Fitzpatrick. The Bidwell/Bartleson party were grateful to travel over one thousand miles of the Oregon/California Trail with the Jesuits and their experienced guide, until the parting of the ways at Soda Springs. Half of Bidwell's company here changed their distination to Oregon. Those who stayed on for California established the main route to be followed by emigrants thereafter : along the Humboldt River, through the Sierra Nevada Mountains, and into the Sacramento Valley, with Sutter's Fort (on the present site of Sacramento) as the target. The difficulties that confronted Bidwell's party, and the problems and experiences of the journey, were to be echoed again and again in later migrations, for which it became the prototype. Leadership and discipline posed a problem, as for many subsequent caravans. John Bartleson was not the best man for the captaincy, which was never at any stage a happy one. He and his eight followers had refused to travel unless he was given the post. Bidwell was appointed secretary. Before the journey was over Bartleson was to moan : 'If ever I get back to Missouri, I would gladly eat out of the troughs with my pigs.' Bidwell —young, robust, resourceful, the stuff of pioneers—was indefatigable in seeing the journey through, and proved the superior leader. A publisher in Missouri had asked him to keep a journal of the journey. It is the only detailed chronicle of the 1841 migration, and was later written up into the account chiefly quoted here.

Five of the party were women. Two unattached women found partners and were married on the trail : one a daughter of the migrating Williams family, the other a widow with one son. Nancy Kelsey, wife of Benjamin, had a small daughter, and was the only woman to stay on for California.

On 12 May the company set off, following the well-marked trading trail to Santa Fé for two days, before turning off on to the thinly tracked route to Fort Laramie. On 17 May Indians ferried them across the Kansas River on 'bull boats'—buffalo hides stretched over wooden frames. The missionaries had four carts, each drawn by two mules in tandem. Behind came eight wagons drawn by mules or horses. Bringing up the rear were six wagons pulled by the slower moving oxen. Fitzpatrick moved ahead each day and selected a camping site for the night.

For a time, till we reached the Platte River, one day was much like another [*wrote Bidwell*]. We set forth every morning and camped every night, detailing men to stand guard. Captain Fitzpatrick and the missionary party would generally take the lead and we would follow. Fitzpatrick knew all about the Indian tribes, and when there was any danger we kept in a more compact body, to protect one another. At other times we would be scattered along, sometimes for half a mile or more. We were generally together, because there was often work to be done to avoid delay. We had to make the road, frequently digging down steep banks, filling gulches, removing stones, etc. In such cases everybody would take a spade or do something to help make the roads passable. When we camped at night we usually drew the wagons and carts together in a hollow square and picketed our animals inside the corral. The wagons were common ones and of no special pattern, and some of them were covered. The tongue of one would be fastened to the back of another. To lessen the danger from Indians, we usually had no fires at night and did our cooking in the daytime.[5]

The first major incident the company had was a scare from a party of Cheyenne Indians shortly before reaching the Platte River, about two weeks after setting out.

One of our men who chanced to be out hunting, some distance from the company and behind us, suddenly appeared without mule, gun, or pistol, and lacking most of his clothes, and in great excitement reported that he had been surrounded by thousands of Indians. The company, too, became excited, and Fitzpatrick tried, but with little effect, to control and pacify them. Every man started his team into a run, till the oxen, like the mules and horses, were in full gallop. Captain Fitzpatrick went ahead and directed them to follow, and as fast as they came to the bank of the river he put the wagons in the form of a hollow square, and had all the animals securely picketed within. After awhile the Indians came in sight. There were only forty of them, but they were well mounted on horses and were evidently a war party, for they had no women except one, a medicine woman. They came up and camped within one hundred yards of us on the river below. Fitzpatrick told us that they would not have come in that way if they were hostile. . . . When the Indians had put up their lodges, Fitzpatrick and John Gray . . . went out to them and by signs were made to understand that the Indians did not intend to hurt the man or take his mule or gun, but that he was so excited when he saw them that they had to disarm him to keep him from shooting them; they did not know what had become of his pistol or of his clothes, which they said he had thrown off. They surrendered the mule and gun, thus showing that they were friendly. They proved to be Cheyenne Indians. Ever afterwards the man went by the name of Cheyenne Dawson.[5]

The Protestant faith was now officially represented in the company in the form of a lively sixty-four-years-old Methodist preacher called Joseph Williams, who, riding alone, had overtaken the caravan on 26 May. His evangelical faith injected courage, and he had physical as well as moral toughness. But, he admits in his journal, he had been relieved when he heard from some Indians that a company of white people was a short distance ahead.

I could scarcely follow the wagon tracks, the ground was so hard in the prairie. I had almost concluded, at last, to turn back, and got down on my knees, and asked the Lord whether I should do so or not. These words came to my mind: 'The Lord shall be with thee, and no hand shall harm thee.' I then renewed my resolution to go on in the name of the Lord, believing that all would be well, and that I should, in the end, return safely home. I went cheerfully for some time; but was occasionally perplexed with doubts. About an hour before sunset, I got down off my horse and prayed again. God renewed the promise, and I got up and started on, refreshed in spirit, and with renewed courage, thinking all would be well; and instead of sleeping in the prairie, I got to an encampment where there was fire, and plenty of wood, and good water, and I praised God with all my heart. I roasted my meat, sweetened some water, and, with my biscuits, made a hearty supper; laid down by my fire, and slept well and comfortably till morning. A little dog that the company had left, kept around the camp, barking and howling.

Next morning . . . I crossed the Vermillion Creek, and arose on the rolling prairie. I shouted some hours over these beautiful plains. . . . Not an Indian appeared that day. About 4 o'clock in the afternoon, I saw the company about four miles ahead, but soon lost sight of them again; and coming to the place where the compnay had stopped to eat dinner, I alighted, and let my horse feed awhile. At this place, as the company afterwards told me, about two hundred Indians had been seen only an hour before. They had sometimes hung on the rear of the company, and had made some show of attacking those who lingered behind the main body. . . . The company said it was ninety-nine chances to one that I escaped the hands of the Indians, for they had been seen all along where I had come. Surely a wise God controlled the heathens, and protected me; . . . One of the company was a Catholic priest, a Mr. de Smidt [*Father de Smet*], who was extremely kind to me, and invited me to come and eat supper with him that night, and next morning brought me some venison. He appeared to be a very fine man. I was invited to sing by a woman, and then to pray. I did so.[45]

Not everyone in the party wished to be preached to. Williams was soon complaining in his journal:

On Sunday, 30th [*May*], I had a thought of trying to preach to the company. There were some as wicked people among them as I ever saw in all my life. There was some reluctance shown by the captain of the company; others wanted me to preach to them. . . . Col. Bartleson had been a Methodist, but is now a backslider. Our leader, Fitzpatrick, is a wicked, worldly man, and is much opposed to missionaries going among the Indians. He has some intelligence, but is deistical in his principles. . . .[45]

But one couple at least was grateful for the preacher's presence. Williams performed a marriage ceremony of doubtful legality near the Blue River. Bidwell recorded in his journal:

Wonderful! this evening a new family was created! Isaac Kelsey was married to Miss Williams, daughter of R. Williams. The marriage service was performed by the Rev. P. R. Williams, so now we have five families if we include a widow and child.[4]

The sophisticated Jesuit, Father de Smet, was baffled, but at the same time amused, by the unsophisticated preacher, Williams, and wrote:

. . . he wished some religion, it being well understood that his was the best. I say *his*, because he was neither *a* Methodist, *a* Protestant, nor *a* Catholic—not even a Christian; he maintained that a Jew, a

Turk, or an idolater may be as agreeable as any other in the sight of God. For the proof of his doctrine he relied (strange to say) on the authority of St. Paul, and particularly on this text: *Unus Dominus una fides* [One Lord, one faith]. In fact, these were the very words with which he greeted us, the first time we saw him, and which formed the subject of a long valedictory discourse that he delivered in one of the meeting houses of Westport, previous to his departure for his western mission. By whom was he sent? We have never ascertained. . . . He carried his absurdities and contradictions so far, that he excited the hilarity of the whole camp. His ingenuous simplicity was even greater than his tolerance. . . .[17]

Williams's diary entry for 26 April 1841 reveals that a personal impulse had brought the old preacher to the Oregon Trail:

This morning I started from my residence, near Napoleon, Ripley county, Indiana, for the Oregon Territory, on the Columbia River, west of the Rocky Mountains; though many of my friends tried to dissuade me from going, telling me of the many dangers and difficulties I should have to go through, exposed to hostile Indians and wild beasts, and also on account of my advanced age, being at this time in my 64th year. But my mind leads me strongly to go; I want to preach to the people there, and also to the Indians, as well as to see the country. I try to put my trust in the God of heaven, who rules the earth, and seas, and mountains, and the savage tribes, and all the wild beasts of the forest, and the storms, and all the poisonous vapors of the earth and air; who preserves all who put their trust in him. My soul seems wholly resigned to his will in all things, whether to live or die, to prosper or suffer. All is right that the Lord doeth; why then should we fear? So I bade my children and friends farewell, not knowing that I should ever see them again in this world. Lord, keep us near thee![45]

Buffaloes provided meat for the Bidwell/Bartleson party, as they were to do for subsequent emigrant companies.

Bidwell:

Before reaching the Platte we had seen an abundance of antelopes and elk, prairie wolves and villages of prairie dogs, but only an occasional buffalo. We now began to kill buffaloes for food, and at the suggestion of John Gray, and following the practice of Rocky Mountain white hunters, our people began to kill them just to get the tongues and marrow bones, leaving all the rest of the meat on the plains for the wolves to eat. But the Cheyenne, who traveled ahead of us for two or three days, set us a better example. At their camps we noticed that when they killed buffaloes they took all the meat, everything but the bones. . . . There is no better beef in the world than that of the buffalo; it is also very good jerked—cut into strings and thoroughly dried. It was an easy matter to kill buffaloes after we got to where they were numerous, by keeping out of sight and to the leeward of them. I think I can truthfully say that I saw in that region in one day more buffaloes than I have ever seen of cattle in all my life. I have seen the plains black with them for several days' journey as far as the eye could reach. They seemed to be coming northward continually from the distant plains to the Platte to get water, and would plunge in and swim across by thousands—so numerous that they changed not only the color of the water, but its taste, until it was unfit to drink—but we had to use it.

One night when we were encamped on the south fork of the Platte they came in such droves that we had to sit up and fire guns and make what fires we could to keep them from running over us and trampling us into the dust. We were obliged to go out some distance from the camp to turn them; Captain Fitzpatrick told us that if we did not do this the buffaloes in front could not turn aside for the pressure of those behind. We could hear them thundering all night long; the ground fairly trembled with vast approaching bands, and if they had not been diverted, wagons, animals, and emigrants would have been trodden under their feet. One cannot nowadays describe the rush and wildness of the thing. A strange feature was that when old oxen, tired and sore-footed, got among a buffalo herd, as they sometimes would in the night, they would soon become as wild as the wildest buffalo; and if ever recovered, it was because they could not run so fast as the buffaloes or one's horse. The ground over which the herds traveled was left rather barren, but buffalo grass being short and curling, in traveling over it they did not cut it up as much as they would other kinds.[5]

Fatal gunshot accidents became a recurring feature of emigrant companies travelling on the Oregon/California Trail. The prototype was described by Bidwell in his journal, 13 June :

A mournful accident occurred in the Camp this morning—a young man by the name of Shotwell while in the act of taking a gun out of the wagon, drew it, with the muzzle towards him in such a manner that it went off and shot him near the heart—he lived about an hour and died in the full possession of his senses.[4]

Sudden storms, with heavy rains, were customary on the plains, and on a very hot day on the Platte River the emigrants were startled by the spectacle of a cyclone, here described by Father de Smet :

Once as the storm was raging near us, we witnessed a sublime sight. A spiral abyss seemed to be suddenly formed in the air. The clouds followed each other into it with such velocity, that they attracted all objects around them, whilst such clouds as were too large and too far distant to feel its influence turned in an opposite direction. The noise we heard in the air was like that of a tempest. On beholding the conflict we fancied that all the winds had been let loose from the four points of the compass. It is very probable that if it had approached much nearer, the whole caravan would have made an ascension into the clouds, . . . The spiral column moved majestically toward the North, and alighted on the surface of the Platte. Then, another scene was exhibited to our view. The waters, agitated by its powerful action, began to turn round with a frightful noise, and were suddenly drawn up to the clouds in a spiral form. The column appeared to measure a mile in height; and such was the violence of the winds which came down in a perpendicular direction, that in the twinkling of an eye the trees were torn and uprooted, and their boughs scattered in every direction. But what is violent does not last. After a few minutes, the frightful visitation ceased. The column, not being able to sustain the weight at its base was dissolved almost as quickly as it had been formed. Soon after the sun re-appeared: all was calm and we pursued our journey.[17]

In a letter written on the trail, dated 14 July, Father de Smet described the nature of the countryside the party had traversed.

With the exception of the mounds which run parallel to each other

on both sides of the Platte river, and after passing under the Black
Hills, disappear at the base of the Rocky Mountains, the whole plain
which we traversed for 1500 miles after we had left Westport, might
be called the Prairie Ocean. In fact, nearly the whole of this territory
is of an undulating form, and the undulations resemble the billows of
the sea when agitated by the storm. On the tops of some of these
elevations we have seen shells and petrifactions, such as are found on
several mountains in Europe. . . .

In proportion as one removes from the banks of the Missouri or
penetrates into the Western regions, the forests lose much in height,
density and depth, in consequence of the scarcity of water. Soon
after, only the rivers are lined with narrow skirts of wood, in which
are seldom seen any lofty creeks. In the neighborhood of creeks and
rivulets we generally find willow bushes, and where there is no water
it would be vain to look for any thing but grass, and even this grass is
only found in the fertile plains that lie between Westport and the
Platte river.

This intimate connexion between rivers and forests is so striking
to the eye, that our beasts of burden had not journeyed more than
eight days through this desert, when we saw them in some manner
exult and double their pace at the sight of the trees that appeared
at a distance. This was chiefly observable when the day's journey
had been rather long. This scarcity of wood in the western regions,
so much at variance with what is seen in other parts of North
America, proceeds from two principal causes. In the plains on this
side of Platte river, from the custom which the Indians who live here
have adopted, to fire their prairies towards the end of autumn, in
order to have better pasture at the return of spring; but in the Far
West, where the Indians do not follow this practice, (because they
fear to drive away the animals that are necessary for their subsistence,
or to expose themselves to be discovered by the strolling parties of
their enemies,) it proceeds from the nature of the soil, which being a
mixture of sand and light earth, is every where so very barren
that with the exception of the absynth that covers the plains,
and the gloomy verdure that shades the mountains, vegetation
is confined to the vicinity of rivers,—a circumstance which

renders a journey through the Far West extremely long and tedious.[17]

Of the oddly-shaped mounds along the Platte River, Father de Smet was most fascinated by Chimney Rock.

It is called so on account of its extraordinary form; but instead of applying to it an appellation which is rather unworthy this wonder of nature, . . . it would have been more proper to call it 'the inverted funnel', as there is no object which it resembles more. Its whole height, including the base, body and column, is scarce less than four or five hundred feet; the column or chimney is only about one hundred and thirty feet high, so that there is nothing striking in the loftiness of its dimensions. But what excites our astonishment, is the manner in which this remnant of a mountain, composed of sand and clay, has been so shaped, and how it has for such a length of time preserved this form, in spite of the winds that are so violent in these parts. . . . The chimney is not the only remarkable mound to be met with in this vast solitude. There are many others of various forms. One is called 'The House', another 'The Castle', a third 'The Fort', &c. And, in fact, if a traveller was not convinced that he journeys through a desert, where no other dwellings exist but the tents put up at night and removed in the morning, he would be induced to believe them so many ancient fortresses or Gothic castles and with a little imagination, based upon some historical knowledge, he might think himself transported amid the ancient mansions of Knight errantry. On one side are seen large ditches, and high walls; on the other, avenues, gardens and orchards; farther on, parks, ponds, and lofty trees. Sometimes the fancy presents a castle of the middle ages, and even conjures up the lord of the manor; but instead of all these magnificent remains of antiquity, we find only barren mounds on all sides, filled with cliffs formed by the falling of the waters, serving as dens to an infinite number of rattle snakes and other venomous reptiles.[17]

An incident mentioned by Bidwell reveals that in the clear atmosphere of this region distances could prove deceptive.

Above the junctions of the forks of the Platte we continued to pass notable natural formations – first O'Fallon's Bluffs, then Court House Rocks, a group of fantastic shapes to which some of our party started to go. After they had gone what seemed fifteen or twenty miles the huge pile looked just as far off as when they had started, and so they turned and came back. . . .[5]

On 22 June they reached the small fur-trading post of Fort Laramie. They had been forty-two days on the trail, averaging fifteen miles a day. It was a fast rate and wearing on the ox-teams who were yoked nine or ten hours a day. Fitzpatrick was hired by the missionaries and his pace was geared to that of the lighter carts of his group. At one stage the travellers to California held a meeting to decide whether or not to drop behind. They decided they could not afford to lose the services of so experienced a guide and kept up a rate of progress that was faster than many trains of later years, whose wagons, however, were probably carrying heavier loads.

On leaving Fort Laramie the trail became rougher, passing through the Black Hills darkened by pines and cedars. The North Fork of the Platte River, swift and turbulent, presented a fording problem on 1 July. A wagon overturned and a mule was carried away and drowned. Fifty miles farther on they passed Independence Rock, over the years to become profusely marked by various means with the names of passing emigrants. It became customary, too, to climb the rock for the panoramic view. Then along the valley of the Sweetwater, with exciting new natural sights like the Devil's Gate, where the river thrust between high cliffs, and on to the gradual climb of the South Pass, a wide opening through the Rocky Mountains.

Bidwell:

As we ascended the Platte, buffaloes became scarcer, and on the Sweetwater none were to be seen. Now appeared in the distance to the north and west, gleaming under the mantle of perpetual snow, the lofty range known as the Wind River Mountains. It was the first time I had seen snow in summer; some of the peaks were very precipitous, and the view was altogether most impressive. Guided by Fitzpatrick, we crossed the Rockies at or near the South Pass, where the mountains were apparently low. Some years before a man named William Sublette, an Indian fur trader, went to the Rocky Mountains with goods in wagons, and those were the only wagons that had ever been there before us; sometimes we came across the tracks, but generally they were obliterated and thus were of no service.[5]

*Even during the summer months it could be very cold at night on the
trail. A few days before the train reached South Pass old Williams
wrote in his journal:*

At night we were cold. I could not keep warm, although I had a
buffalo robe to cover me. It is said here, that the ground is sometimes
frozen in August an inch deep. Today we traveled over some high,
bald hills; dined on good fat buffalo, that our hunters had just killed.
We went over on Sweet River and dried our meat for the remaining
part of our journey, where we expected not to find any more game.
We are still in sight of the big Wind Mountain; for it may be seen at
the distance of seventy or eighty miles. For hundreds of miles we
have to pass over barren ground. I went out with the hunters to bring
in meat to dry and we soon killed a buffalo. . . . The next day we came
in sight of the Sweet River Mountain. Its peaks were tolerably well
whitened with snow. There are some white bears in these mountains,
but we have not killed any yet. There are also some white wolves,
about as white as sheep. They are a dull, sleepy looking animal, and
very surly; not very mindful of any thing, nor much afraid.[45]

*On 23 July the caravan reached Green River, which they easily
forded. Here they met a party of sixty trappers, and camped for a day.
It was perhaps the last great trapper rendezvous. The emigrants traded
alcohol for clothes, moccasins, and dressed skins. The trappers' advice
was not encouraging. It was their opinion that wagons might get through
to Oregon, by going along the Snake River – but they did not think it
possible to take wagons into California. Seven men in the emigrant
party decided to turn back to Missouri; others changed their destination
from California to Oregon.*

*On 30 July the only unattached woman now in the company was
married. This time Father de Smet officiated, confident in the authority
vested in him by the historic Church.*

Again Bidwell recorded the event with enthusiasm:

Guess what took place; another family was created! Widow Gray,
who was a sister to Mrs Kelsey, was married to a man who joined
our Company at Fort Laramie, his right name I forget; but
his everywhere name in the mountains, was Cocrun. He had but

one eye – marriage ceremony performed by Father De Smet.[4]

At Soda Springs the company broke up into those heading north-west to Fort Hall and on to Oregon, and those determined to reach California.

John Bidwell:

At Soda Springs – at the northernmost bend of Bear River – our party separated. It was a bright and lovely place. The abundance of soda water, including the intermittent gushing so-called Steamboat Spring; the beautiful fir and cedar covered hills; the huge piles of red or brown sinter, the result of fountains once active but then dry – all these, together with the river, lent a charm to its wild beauty and made the spot a notable one. Here the missionary party were to turn north and go into the Flathead nation. Fort Hall, about forty miles distant on Snake River, lay on their route. There was no road, but something like a trail, doubtless used by trappers, led in that direction. From Fort Hall there was also a trail down Snake River, by which trapping parties reached the Columbia River and Fort Vancouver, the headquarters of the Hudson's Bay Company.

Our party, originally sixty-nine, had become lessened to sixty-four in number. One had accidentally shot and killed himself at the forks of the Platte. Another of our party, named Simpson, had left us at Fort Laramie. Three had turned back from Green River, intending to make their way to Fort Bridger and await an opportunity to return home. . . . Thirty-two of our party, becoming discouraged, decided not to venture without path or guide into the unknown and trackless regions toward California, but concluded to go with the missionary party to Fort Hall and thence find their way down the Snake and Columbia rivers into Oregon. The rest of us – also thirty-two in number, including Benjamin Kelsey, his wife and little daughter – remained firm, refusing to be diverted from our original purpose of going direct to California. After getting all the information we could from Captain Fitzpatrick, we regretfully bade good-bye to our fellow emigrants and to Father De Smet and his party.

We were now thrown entirely upon our own resources. All the country beyond was to us a veritable *terra incognita*, and we only knew that California lay to the west. Captain Fitzpatrick was not much better informed, but he had heard that parties penetrated the country to the southwest and west of Salt Lake to trap for beaver; and by his advice four of our men went with the parties to Fort Hall to consult Captain Grant, who was in charge there, and gain information. Meanwhile our depleted party slowly made its way down the west side of Bear River.[5]

Thousands of emigrants were to profit from the experience of this group who stayed firm in their resolve to reach California. Father de Smet admired their grit, saying that they 'were pursuing their enterprise with the constancy which is characteristic of Americans'. None of the party had experience of the trails, but they had the right qualities to succeed in their enterprise. They were nearly all of farmer stock. Roughest and toughest characters were the Kelsey brothers, Benjamin and Andrew, from Kentucky, and another Kentuckian was Grove Cook, whose wife, not travelling, was of the Sublette fur-trading family. Bidwell and Nicholas Dawson were of an age, and had both been schoolteachers, moving along the frontier territories. The latter had decided on five years' travel before settling down. Bidwell described James Johns as being the most fearless man he had known. There were a few Germans. Joseph B. Chiles used the experience gained in '41 to lead an emigrant party across the continent in '43. James Springer also guided other parties. Young Talbot Green carried medical supplies and acted as doctor. Though well-liked, he was noticeably silent about his past, and he gave no explanation as to why he was carrying a large lump of lead. Nancy Kelsey, wife of Benjamin, earned a place in the pioneering history of America, as did baby Ann, about one year old. The others with families who had originally set out had chosen the Oregon journey. The party for California had nine wagons, drawn by tired mules or oxen, and some saddle horses. In moving south down Bear Valley towards Great Salt Lake they were moving into difficult desert country.

With Father de Smet and the Rev. Joseph Williams on the trail to Fort Hall, our story remains solely with the pen of John Bidwell. During the first day after the separation at Soda Springs the emigrants for California travelled about ten miles, before camping on Bear River. Here Bidwell's youthful exuberance was displayed by his setting off with James Johns to reach and touch snow on the mountains.

So, without losing time to get our guns or coats or give notice at the camp, we started direct for the snow, with the impression that we could go and return by sundown. But there intervened a range of low mountains, a certain peak of which seemed almost to touch the snow. Both of us were fleet of foot and made haste, but we only gained the summit of the peak before sundown. The distance must have been twelve or fifteen miles. A valley intervened and the snow lay on a higher mountain beyond. I proposed to camp, but Jimmy gave me a disdainful look, as much as to say: 'You are afraid to go', and quickened his gait into a run down the mountain toward the snow. I called to him to stop, but he would not even look back. A firm resolve seized me – to overtake him, but not again to ask him to return. We crossed the valley in the night, saw many camp fires, and gained a sharp ridge leading up to the snow. This was first brushy and then rocky. The brush had no paths except those made by wild animals. The rocks were sharp and cut through our moccasins and made our feet bleed. But up and up we went until long after midnight, and until a cloud covered the mountain. We were above the timber line, except a few stunted fir trees, under which we crawled to await for day, for it was too dark to see. Day soon dawned, but we were almost frozen. Our fir tree nest had been the lair of grizzly bears that had wallowed there and shed quantities of shaggy hair. The snow was still beyond, and we had lost both sight and direction. But in an hour or two we reached it. It was nearly as hard as ice.

Filling a handkerchief, without taking time to admire the scenery, we started toward the camp by a new route, for our feet were too sore to go by the way of the rocky ridge by which we had come. But the new way led into trouble. There were thickets so dense as to exclude the sun, and roaring little streams in deep, dark chasms. We had to crawl through paths which looked untrodden except by grizzlies. . . . We carried our drawn butcher knives in our hands, for they were our only weapons. At last we emerged into the valley. Apparently numerous Indians had left that very morning, as shown by the tracks of lodge poles drawn on the ground. Making haste, we soon gained the hills, and at about 2 P.M. sighted our wagons, already two or three miles on the march. When our friends saw us they stopped, and all who could ran to welcome us. They had given us up for lost, supposing that we had been killed by the hostile Blackfeet, . . .[5]

The train had advanced a little over a hundred miles towards Salt Lake when the men who had gone to Fort Hall brought the information . . .

. . . that we must strike out west of Salt Lake – as it was even then called by the trappers – being careful not to go too far south, lest we should get into a wasteless country without grass. They also said we must be careful not to go too far north, lest we should get into a broken country and steep cañons, and wander about, as trapping parties had been known to do, and become bewildered and perish.

September had come before we reached Salt Lake, which we struck at its northern extremity. Part of the time we had purposely traveled slowly to enable the men from Fort Hall the sooner to overtake us. But unavoidable delays were frequent; daily, often hourly. Indian fires obscured mountains and valleys in a dense, smoky atmosphere, so that we could not see any considerable distance in order to avoid obstacles. The principal growth, on plain and hill alike, was the interminable sagebrush, and often it was difficult, for miles at a time, to break a road through it, and sometimes a lightly laden wagon would be overturned. Its monotonous dull color and scraggy appearance gave a most dreary aspect to the landscape. But it was not wholly useless. Where large enough it made excellent fuel, and it was the home and shelter of the hare – generally known as the jackrabbit – and of the sage hen. Trees were almost a sure sign of water in that region. But the mirage was most deceptive, magnifying stunted sagebrush or diminutive hillocks into trees and groves. Thus misled, we traveled all day without water, and at midnight found ourselves in a plain as level as a floor, incrusted with salt and as white as snow. Crusts of salt broken up by our wagons and driven by the chilly night wind like ice on the surface of the water of a frozen pond was to me the striking counterfeit of a winter scene.

This plain became softer and softer until our poor, almost famished animals could not pull our wagons. In fact, we were going direct to Salt Lake and did not know it. So, in search of water, we turned from a southerly to an easterly course, and went about ten miles, and soon after daylight arrived at Bear River. So near Salt Lake were we that the water in the river was too salty for us or our animals to use, but we had to use it. It would not quench thirst, but it did save life. The grass looked most luxuriant, and sparkled as if covered with frost, but it was salt. Our hungry, jaded animals refused to eat it, and we had to lie by a whole day to rest them before we could travel.

Leaving this camp and bearing northwest we crossed our tracks on the salt plain, having thus described a triangle of several miles in dimensions. One of the most serious of our troubles was to find water where we could camp at night. So soon came another hot day and all night without water. From a westerly course we turned directly north, and guided by antelope trails, came in a few miles to an abundance of grass and good water. The condition of our animals compelled us to rest here nearly a week. Meanwhile two of our men who had been to Fort Hall went ahead to explore. Provisions were becoming scarce, and we saw we must avoid unnecessary delay. The two men were gone about five days. Under their lead we set forth, bearing west, then southwest, around Salt Lake, then again west. After two or three fatiguing days – one day and night without water – the first notice we had of approach to any considerable mountain was the sight of crags dimly seen through the smoke, many hundred feet above our heads. Here was plenty of good grass and water. Nearly all now said: 'Let us leave our wagons, otherwise the snows will overtake us before we get to California.' So we stopped one day and threw away everything we could not carry, made pack saddles, and packed the oxen, mules, and horses, and started.[5]

Unfortunately, none of the men was familiar with the art of packing.

The trouble began the very first day. But we started – most of us on foot, for nearly all the animals, including several of the oxen, had to carry packs. It was but a few minutes before the packs began to turn; horses became scared, mules kicked, oxen jumped and bellowed, and articles were scattered in all directions. We took more pains, fixed things, made a new start, and did better, though packs continued occasionally to fall off and delay us.

Those who had better pack saddles and had tied their loads securely were ahead, while the others were obliged to lag behind because they had to repack, and sometimes things would be strewn all along the route. The first night I happened to be among those who kept pretty well back because the horses out-traveled the oxen. The foremost came to a place and stopped where there was no water or grass, and built a fire so that we could see it and come up to them. We got there about midnight, but some of our oxen that had packs on had not come up, and among them were my two. So I had to return the next morning and find them, Cheyenne Dawson alone volunteering to go with me. One man had brought along about a quart of water, which was carefully doled out before we started, each receiving a little canister cover full – less than half a gill; but as Dawson and I had to go for the oxen we were given a double portion. This was all the water I had until the next day. It was a burning hot day. We could not find the trail of the oxen for a long time, and Dawson refused to go any farther, saying that there were plenty of cattle in California; but I had to do it for the oxen were carrying our provisions and other things. Afterwards I struck the trail and found that the oxen instead of going west had gone north, and I followed them until nearly sundown. They had gone into a grassy country, which showed that they were nearing water. Seeing Indian tracks on their trail following them, I felt there was imminent danger, and at once examined my gun and pistols to see that they were primed and ready. But I soon found my oxen lying down in tall grass by the side of the trail.

Seeing no Indians, I hastened to fasten the packs and make my way to overtake the company. They had promised to stop when they came to water and wait for me. I traveled all night, and at early dawn came to where there was plenty of water and where the company had taken their dinner the day before, but they had failed to stop for me according to promise. I was much perplexed, because I had seen many fires during the night which I took to be Indian fires, so I fastened my oxen to a scraggy willow and began to make circles around to see which way the company had gone. The ground was so hard that the animals had made no impression, which bewildered me. Finally, while making a circle of about three miles off to the south, I saw two men coming on horseback. In the glare of the mirage, which distorted everything, I could not tell whether they were Indians or white men, but I could only tell by the motion that they were mounted. I made a bee-line to my oxen, so as to make breastworks of them. In doing this I came to a small stream, resembling running water, into which I urged my horse, whereupon he went down into a quagmire, over head and ears, out of sight. My gun also went under the mire. I got hold of something on the bank, threw out my gun, which was full of mud and water, and holding to the rope attached to my horse, by dint of hard pulling I succeeded in getting him out – a very sorry sight, his ears and eyes full of mud, his body covered with it. At last, just in time, I was able to move and get behind the oxen. My gun was in no condition to shoot. However, putting dry powder in the pan I determined to do my best in case the supposed Indians should come up; but lo! they were two of our party, coming to meet me, bringing water and provisions. It was a great relief. I felt indignant that the party had not stopped for me – not the less when I learned that Captain Bartleson had said, when they started back to find me, that they 'would be in better business to go ahead and look for a road'. . . .[5]

It was with feelings of immense relief that the party finally came out on the river which J. C. Frémont in 1845 named the Humboldt, but which in 1841 was known to mountain men as either Mary's or Ogden's River.

Our course was first westward and then southward, following this river for many days, till we came to its Sink, near which we saw a solitary horse, an indication that trappers had sometime been in that vicinity. We tried to catch him but failed; he had been there long enough to become very wild. We saw many Indians on the Humboldt, especially toward the Sink. There were many tule marshes. The tule is a rush, large, but here not very tall. It was generally completely covered with honeydew, but this in turn was wholly covered with a pediculous-looking insect which fed upon it. The Indians gathered quantities of the honey and pressed it into balls about the size of one's fist, having the appearance of wet bran. At first we greatly relished this Indian food, but when we saw what it was made of – that the insects pressed into the mass were the main ingredient we lost our appetites and bought no more of it.

From the time we left our wagons many had to walk, and more and more as we advanced. Going down the Humboldt, at least half were on foot. Provisions had given out, except a little coarse green grass among the willows. . . .

On the Humboldt we had a further division of our ranks. In going down the river we went sometimes on one side and sometimes on the other, but mostly on the north side, till we were nearing what are now known as the Humboldt Mountains. We were getting tired, and some were in favor of leaving the oxen, of which we then had only about seven or eight, and rushing on into California. They said there was plenty of beef in California. But some of us said: 'No, our oxen are now our only supply of food. We are doing well, making eighteen or twenty miles a day.' One morning when it was my turn at driving the oxen, the captain traveled so fast that I could not keep up, and was left far behind. When night came I had to leave the trail and go over a rocky declivity for a mile and a half into a gloomy, damp bottom, and unpack the oxen and turn them out to eat, sleeping myself without blankets. I got up the next morning, hunted the oxen out of the willow thicket, and repacked them. Not having had supper or breakfast, and having to travel nine miles before I overtook the party, perhaps I was not in the best humor.

They were waiting, and for the very good reason that they could have nothing to eat till I came up with the oxen and one could be killed. I felt badly treated, and let the captain know it plainly; but, much to my surprise, he made no reply, and none of his men said a word. We killed an ox, ate our breakfast, and got ready to start about one or two o'clock in the afternoon. When nearly ready to go, the captain and one or two of his mess came to us and said: 'Boys, our animals are much better than yours, and we always get out of meat before any of the rest of you. Let us have the most of the meat this time, and we will pay you back the next ox we kill.' We gladly let them have all they wished. But as soon as they had taken it and were mounted ready to start, the captain in a loud voice exclaimed: 'Now we have been found fault with long enough, and we are going to California. If you can keep up with us, all right; if you cannot, you may go to—'; and away they started, the captain and eight men. One of the men would not go with the captain; he said: 'The captain is wrong, and I will stay with you boys.'

In a short time they were out of sight. We followed their trail for two or three days, but after they had crossed over to the south side of the Humboldt and turned south we came into a sandy waste where the wind had entirely obliterated their tracks. We were then thrown entirely upon our own resources. It was our desire to make as great speed as possible westward, deviating only when obstacles interposed, and in such a case bearing south instead of north, so as to be found in a lower latitude in the event that winter should overtake us in the mountains.[5]

In crossing the Humboldt they had missed the luxuriant Truckee Meadows, a much appreciated resting place for later emigrants.

So, perforce, we followed down to the Sink of the Humboldt and were obliged to drink its water, which in the fall of the year becomes stagnant and the color of lye, and not fit to drink or use unless boiled. Here we camped. Leaving the Sink of the Humboldt, we crossed a considerable stream which must have been Carson River, and came to another stream which must have been the Walker River, and followed it up to where it came out of the mountains, which proved to be the Sierra Nevadas. We did not know the name of the mountains. Neither had these rivers then been named, nor had they been seen by Kit Carson or Joe Walker, for whom they were named, nor were they seen until 1845 by Frémont, who named them.

We were now camped on Walker River, at the very eastern base of the Sierra Nevadas, and had only two oxen left. We sent men ahead to see if it would be possible to scale the mountains, while we killed the better of the two oxen and dried the meat in preparation for the ascent. The men returned toward evening and reported that they thought it would be possible to ascend the mountains, though very difficult. We had eaten our supper and were ready for the climb in the morning. Looking back on the plains we saw something coming, which we decided to be Indians. They traveled very slowly, and it was difficult to understand their movements. To make a long story short, it was the eight men that had left us nine days before.

They had gone farther south than we, and had come to a lake, probably Carson Lake, and there had found Indians, who supplied them plentifully with fish and pine nuts. Fish caught in such water are not fit to eat at any time, much less in the fall of the year. The men had eaten heartily of fish and pine nuts and had got something akin to cholera morbus. We ran out to meet them and shook hands, and put our frying pans on and gave them the best supper we could. Captain Bartleson, who when we started from Missouri was a portly man, was reduced to half his former girth. He said: 'Boys, if ever I get back to Missouri I will never leave that country. I would gladly eat out of the troughs with my hogs.' He seemed to be heartily sick of his late experience, but that did not prevent him from leaving us twice after that.

We were now in what is at present Nevada, and probably within forty miles of the present boundary of California. We ascended the mountain on the north side of Walker River to the summit, and then struck a stream running west which proved to be the extreme source of the Stanislaus River. We followed it down for several days and finally came to where a branch ran into it, each forming a cañon. The main river flowed in a precipitous gorge, in places apparently a mile deep, and the gorge that came into it was but little less formidable. At night we found ourselves on the extreme point of the promontory between the two, very tired, and with neither grass nor water. We had to stay there that night. Early the next morning two men went down to see if it would be possible to get down through the smaller cañon.[5]

The two men were Bidwell and Jimmy Johns.

The understanding was that when we went down the cañon if it was practicable to get through we were to fire a gun so that all could follow; but if not, we were not to fire, even if we saw game. When Jimmy and I got down about three-quarters of a mile I came to the conclusion that it was impossible to get through and said to him: 'Jimmy, we might as well go back; we can't go here.' 'Yes, we can', said he, and insisting that we could, he pulled out a pistol and fired.

It was an old dragoon pistol, and reverberated like a cannon. I hurried back to tell the company not to come down, but before I reached them the captain and his party had started. I explained, and warned them that they could not get down; but they went on as fast they could go and then were obliged to stay all day and all night to rest the animals, and had to go among the rocks and pick a little grass for them, and go down to the stream through a terrible place in the cañon to bring water up in cups and camp kettles, and some of the men in their boots, to pour down the animals' throats in order to keep them from perishing. Finally, four of them pulling and four pushing a mule, they managed to get them up one by one, and then carried all the things up again on their backs – not an easy job for exhausted men.

In some way, nobody knows how, Jimmy got through that cañon and into the Sacramento Valley. He had a horse with him – an Indian horse that was bought in the Rocky Mountains, and which could come as near climbing a tree as any horse I ever knew. Jimmy was a character. Of all men I have ever known I think he was the most fearless; he had the bravery of a bulldog. He was not seen for two months – until he was found at Sutter's, afterwards known as Sutter's Fort, now Sacramento City. We went on, traveling as near west as we could. When we killed our last ox we shot and ate crows or anything we could kill, and one man shot a wildcat. We could eat anything. One day in the morning I went ahead, on foot of course, to see if I could kill something, it being understood that the company would keep on as near west as possible and find a practicable road. I followed an Indian trail down into the cañon, meeting many Indians on the way up. They did not molest me, but I did not quite like their looks. I went about ten miles down the cañon, then began to think it time to strike north to intersect the trail of the company going west. A most difficult time I had scaling the precipice. Once I threw my gun ahead of me, being unable to hold it and climb, and then was in despair lest I could not get up where it was, but finally I did barely manage to do so, and make my way north. As the darkness came on I was obliged to look down and feel with my feet lest I should pass over the trail of the party without seeing it. ... Of course sleep was impossible, for I had neither blanket nor coat, and burned or froze alternately as I turned from one side to the other

before the small fire which I had built, until morning, when I
started eastward to intersect the trail, thinking the company had
turned north. But I traveled until noon and found no trail; then
striking south, I came to the camp which I had left the previous
morning.

The party had gone, but not where they said they would go; for
they had taken the same trail I followed into the cañon, but had
gone up the south side, which they had found so steep that many
of the poor animals could not climb it and had to be left. When I
arrived, the Indians were there cutting the horses to pieces and
carrying off the meat. My situation, alone among strange Indians
killing our poor horses, was by no means comfortable. Afterwards
we found that these Indians were always at war with the Californians.
They were known as the Horse Thief Indians, and lived chiefly on
horse flesh; they had been in the habit of raiding the ranches even
to the very coast, driving away horses by the hundreds into the
mountains to eat. That night I overtook the party in camp.

A day or two later we came to a place where there was a great
quantity of horse bones, and we did not know what it meant; we
thought that an army must have perished there. They were, of
course, horses that the Indians had driven in and slaughtered. A few
nights later, fearing depredations, we concluded to stand guard –
all but one man, who would not. So we let his two horses roam
where they pleased. In the morning they could not be found. A few
miles away we came to a village; the Indians had fled, but we
found the horses killed and some of the meat roasting on a fire.

We were now on the edge of the San Joaquin Valley, but we did
not even know that we were in California. We could see a range of
moutains lying to the west – the Coast Range – but we could see
no valley. The evening of the day we started down into the valley
we were very tired, and when night came our party was strung along
for three or four miles, and every man slept where darkness overtook
him. He would take off his saddle for a pillow and turn his horse or
mule loose, if he had one. His animal would be too poor to walk away,
and in the morning he would find him, usually within fifty feet. The
jaded horses nearly perished with hunger and fatigue. When we

overtook the foremost of the party the next morning we found they had come to a pond of water, and one of them had killed a fat coyote. When I came up it was all eaten except the lights and the windpipe, on which I made my breakfast.

From that camp we saw timber to the north of us, evidently bordering a stream running west. It turned out to be the stream that we had followed down in the mountains – the Stanislaus River. As soon as we came in sight of the bottom land of the stream we saw an abundance of antelopes and sandhill cranes. We killed two of each the first evening. Wild grapes also abounded. The next day we killed fifteen deer and antelopes, jerked the meat, and got ready to go on, all except the captain's mess of seven or eight, who decided to stay there and lay in meat enough to last them into California. We were really almost down to tidewater, and did not know it. Some thought it was five hundred miles yet to California. But all thought we had to cross at least that range of mountains in sight to the west before entering the promised land, and how many beyond no man could tell. Nearly all thought it best to press on lest snows might overtake us in the mountains before us, as they had already nearly done on the mountains behind us (the Sierra Nevadas). It was now about the first of November. Our party set forth bearing northwest, aiming for a seeming gap north of a high mountain in the chain to the west of us. That mountain we found to be Mount Diablo. At night the Indians attacked the captain's camp and stole all their animals, which were the best in the company, and the next day the men had to overtake us with just what they could carry in their hands.

The next day, judging from the timber we saw, we concluded there was a river to the west. So two men went ahead to see if they could find a trail or a crossing. The timber proved to be along what is now known as the San Joaquin River. We sent two men on ahead to spy out the country. At night one of them returned, saying they came across an Indian on horseback without a saddle, who wore a cloth jacket but no other clothing. From what they could understand the Indian knew Mr. Marsh and had offered to guide them to his place. He plainly said 'Marsh', and of course we supposed it was the Dr. Marsh before referred to who had written the letter to a friend in

Jackson County, Missouri, and so it proved. One man went with the Indian to Marsh's ranch and the other came back to tell us what he had done, with the suggestion that we should go and cross the river (San Joaquin) at the place to which the trail was leading. In that way we found ourselves two days later at Dr. Marsh's ranch, and there we learned that we were really in California and our journey at an end. After six months we had now arrived at the first settlement in California, November 4, 1841.[5]

In the letter published a year before in the St. Louis newspaper 'Dr.' Marsh had written: 'The difficulty of coming here is imaginary.' His sketchy directions had been followed, and they had arrived, even though it had not been without difficulty and their wagons had been abandoned on the route.

Though his visitors infuriated him by killing his best work ox and eating it for breakfast, John Marsh had cause for satisfaction in the arrival of the first overland party from the American east. In the spring of 1842 he wrote to his parents:

A company of about thirty of my old neighbors in Missouri arrived here the first of November last, and some of them are about returning and are the bearers of this. They arrived here directly at my house with no other guide but a letter of mine. From all the numerous letters I have received from various parts of the United States I am satisfied that an immense emigration will soon swarm to this country. I am now fully satisfied that the Anglo-Saxon race of men who inhabit the United States are destined very shortly to occupy this delightful country. A young woman with a little child in her arms came in the company last fall and was about a month in my house. After this, the men ought to be ashamed to think of the difficulties. It is an object I much desire and have long labored for, to have this country inhabited by Americans. It will now soon be realized.[29]

A notably high proportion of the men who crossed overland to California in 1841 attained wealth and distinction. John Bidwell became a wealthy rancher, member of Congress, and ran for President in 1892 as the Prohibition Party candidate. Charles Weber founded the city of Stockton. Josiah Belden became the first mayor of San Jose. Other success stories could be listed. *The map of California has many reminders of the advance guard of overland emigration: Chiles Valley, Kelsey, Thomas, and Weber Creeks, Bidwell Butte, Creek, Lake, Peak, etc. A street in San Francisco was named after Talbot Green, who had acted as doctor for the Bidwell party and carried a huge lump of lead. When a candidate for mayor of San Francisco in 1851, he was accused of being really Paul Geddes, an absconding bank clerk. He took a ship sailing east and did not return to California.*

Manifest Destiny:
The 'Great Emigration' to Oregon,
1843

The widely employed phrase 'Manifest Destiny' was first used by an Irish-American newspaper editor, John L. O'Sullivan, in July 1845, with reference to the United States' proposed annexation of Texas. But the idea and emotion it embodied had already been alive and active for some years. In the mixture of emotions that actuated the men and women who undertook a difficult and arduous journey across the American continent, the feeling and conception that they were fulfilling a national destiny was often a vibrant strand, inculcated by politician and press. It was active in 1843 with regard to the Oregon territory, whose sovereignty was disputed by the United States and Great Britain, and led in some measure to a party of about one thousand people preparing for the east-to-west crossing. As it turned out, it was an historic journey, for by taking wagons for the first time through to the Pacific Northwest they opened the way for greater numbers of emigrants to follow, leading eventually to Oregon becoming American.

Peter Burnett, who took part in the '43 migration, reveals how the idea of 'Manifest Destiny' had been in his mind:

I saw that a great American community would grow up, in the space of a few years, upon the shores of the distant Pacific; and I felt an ardent desire to aid in this most important enterprise. At that time the country was claimed by both Great Britain and the United States; so that the most ready and peaceable way to settle the conflicting and doubtful claims of the two governments was to fill the country with American citizens. If we could only show, by a *practical* test, that American emigrants could safely make their way across the continent to Oregon with their wagons, teams, cattle, and families, then the solution of the question of title to the country was discovered. Of course, Great Britain would not covet a colony settled by American citizens. . . .[10]

During the spring of '43 American newspapers stimulated interest in

Oregon as a place for settlement. The Cleveland Plain Dealer, *8 March,* called Oregon 'a country of the largest liberty, the only known land of equality on the face of the earth'. *The Iowa* Gazette *announced :* 'The Oregon fever is raging in almost every part of the Union. Companies are forming . . .' *And, under the heading* WESTWARD HO!, *the Painesville, Ohio,* Telegraph, *on 24 May, announced :*

The tide of emigration flowing westward this season must be overwhelming. Besides the hundreds and thousands that daily throng the steamboats on the Lakes there is a constant stream of 'movers' on land. From ten to fifteen teams have passed through this town every day for the last three weeks, winding their way to Wisconsin and Iowa, and some, we understand are bound for the 'far west' which in these latter days means a country somewhere between the Rocky Mountains and sundown. Those we noticed had the appearance generally of intelligence, respectability and wealth and gave indication of that enterprising and energetic character which alone takes upon itself the hardships and privations incident to the settlement of a new country.[35]

Having completed my arrangements [*Peter Burnett tells us*], I left my house in Weston [*Platte County*] on the 8th day of May, 1843, with two ox wagons, and one small two-horse wagon, four yoke of oxen, two mules, and a fair supply of provisions; and arrived at the rendezvous, some twelve miles west of Independence, and just beyond the line of the State, on the 17th of May.[10]

An interested observer of the gathering of the emigrants was Matthew C. Field, who was with a hunting party organized by Sir Drummond Stewart, a Scottish aristocrat.

During our detention among the upper settlements, before starting out, a constant source of interest to us was the gathering of people bound to Oregon. One Sunday morning about the usual church hour in a larger place, five or six wagons passed through the town of Westport, and one old man, with silver hair, was with the party. Women and children were walking; fathers and brothers were driving loose cattle or managing the heavy teams; and keen-eyed youngsters, with their chins yet smooth, and rifles on their shoulders,

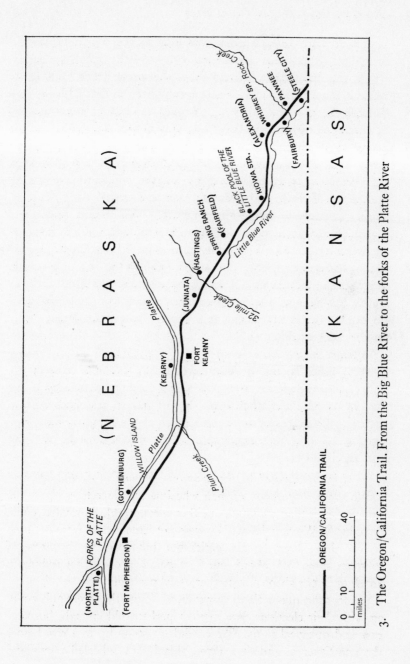

3. The Oregon/California Trail. From the Big Blue River to the forks of the Platte River

kept in advance of the wagons, with long strides, looking as if they were already watching around the corners of the streets for game. There was one striking feature about this party which leads us to name it more particularly. Though travelling on the Sabbath, and through the little town that was all quiet and resting from business in reverence of the day, there was that in the appearance of the people that banished at once even the remotest idea of profanation. They were all clean and evidently apparelled in their best Sunday gear. Their countenances were sedate and the women wore that mild composure of visage – so pleasantly resigned – so eloquent of a calm spirit – so ready to kindle up into smiles – that is seen more often among church-goers, perhaps, than in ball-room or boudoir. Some of the women carried books and the prettiest girl held hers open before her, as she stepped a little coquettishly through the dust of the road. Whether she was reading, or trying, or pretending to read, was hard to tell, but the action had a *naïve* effect, and as she passed she was, no doubt, much astonished at a strange young gentleman, who audibly addressed her with –

'*Nymph, in thy orisons be all my sins remembered!*'

Many other bodies of these adventurous travellers crossed our notice at Independence, Westport, and at encampments made in the vicinity of these and other towns, but in their largest force we saw them just after crossing the Kansas River, about the 1st of June. The Oregonians were assembled here to the number of six or eight hundred . . .[18]

Field was fascinated by the emigrants' manner of electing officers:

We saw a large body of men wheeling and marching about the prairie, describing evolutions neither recognizable as savage, civic, or military. We soon knew they were not Indians and were not long setting them down for the emigrants, but what, in the name of mystery, they were about, our best guessing could not reduce to anything in the shape of a mathematical probability.

On arriving among them, however, we found they were only going on with their elections, in a manner perhaps old enough, but very new and quizzical to us. The candidates stood up in a row before the constituents, and at a given signal they wheeled about and marched off, while the general mass *broke* after them 'lickity-split', each man forming in behind his favourite, so that every candidate flourished a sort of tail of his own, and the man with the longest tail was elected! These proceedings were continued until a Captain and a Council of Ten were elected; and, indeed, if the scene can be conceived, it must appear as a curious mingling of the whimsical with the wild. Here was a congregation of rough, bold and adventurous men, gathered from distant and opposite sections of the Union, just forming an acquaintance with each other, to last, in all probability through good or evil fortune, through the rest of their days. Few of them expected or thought of ever returning to the States again. They had with them their wives and children, and aged, dependent relatives. They were going, with stout and determined hearts to traverse a wild and desolate region, and take possession of a far corner of their country, destined to prove a new and strong arm of a mighty nation. These men were running about the prairie in long strings, the leader, in sport and for the purpose of puzzling the judges, doubling and winding in the drollest fashion – so that the all-important business of forming a government, seemed very much like the merry school-boy game of 'snapping the whip'! It was really very funny to see the candidates for the solemn 'Council of Ten' run several hundred yards away, to show off the length of their tails, and then cut a half circle, so as to turn and admire their longitudinal popularity *in extenso* themselves! 'Running for office' is certainly performed in more literal fashion on the prairie than we see the same sort of business performed in town. . . .[18]

That day the emigrants must have been equally surprised at the sight of a Scottish aristocrat and his party of young gentlemen setting off into the prairie to hunt buffalo.

Peter Burnett:
On the 18th of May the emigrants at the rendezvous held a meeting, and appointed a committee to see Dr. Whitman. . . . The meeting adjourned to meet at the Big Springs . . . On the 20th I attended the meeting at the Big Springs, where I met Colonel John Thornton, Colonel Bartleson, Mr. Rickman, and Dr. Whitman. At this meeting rules and regulations were adopted. . . . it was agreed

in camp that we all should start on Monday morning, May 22. We had delayed our departure, because we thought the grass too short to support our stock. The spring of 1843 was very late, and the ice in the Missouri River at Weston only broke up on the 11th of April.

On the 22nd of May, 1843, a general start was made from the rendezvous, and we reached Elm Grove, about fifteen miles distant, at about 3 P.M. This grove had but two trees, both elms, and some few dogwood bushes, which we used for fuel. The small elm was most beautiful, in the wild and lonely prairie; and the large one had all its branches trimmed off for firewood. The weather being clear, and the road as good as possible, the day's journey was most delightful. The white-sheeted wagons and the fine teams, moving in the wilderness of green prairie, made the most lovely appearance. The place where we encamped was very beautiful; and no scene appeared to our enthusiastic visions more exquisite than the sight of so many wagons, tents, fires, cattle, and people, as were here collected. At night the sound of joyous music was heard in the tents. Our long journey thus began in sunshine and song, in anecdote and laughter; but these all vanished before we reached its termination.

On the 24th we reached the Walkalusia River, where we let our wagons down the steep bank by ropes. On the 26th we reached the Kansas River, and we finished crossing it on the 31st. At this crossing we met Fathers De Smet and De Vos, missionaries to the Flathead Indians. On the 1st of June we organized our company, by electing Peter H. Burnett as Captain, J. W. Nesmith as Orderly Sergeant, and nine councilmen.[10]

The Dr Whitman mentioned, whom the emigrants had been so anxious to meet, was Marcus Whitman, a Presbyterian medical missionary, who, following a visit to the east, was returning to his mission to the Nez Percé Indians. Missionaries shared with fur-traders in opening the way for settlement of the Pacific Northwest. Jason Lee had established a Methodist mission in the Willamette Valley in 1834. And in 1836 Presbyterians Marcus Whitman and Henry Spalding made the overland crossing, actually taking their wives, the first white women to cross the continent. The mission they established at Waiilatpu on the Walla Walla River became a receiving station for parties of immigrants.

(Burnett reveals that Father de Smet, of the Catholic mission to the Flathead Indians, was again on the Oregon Trail.) Whitman played a leading role in the success of the migration of '43, for at Fort Hall, where he was taken on as guide, he insisted, correctly, against contrary advice from fur-traders, that wagons could get through to the Columbia River.

The main party moved west on 22 May, but Whitman did not follow until 1 June, spending that night with the second expeditionary party of government explorer J. C. Frémont. Captain Theodore Talbot, one of Frémont's officers, recorded meeting the missionary on that evening:

Dr. Whitman, the Baptist [*sic*] Missionary established at Walla-wallah on the Columbia, was our guest tonight. He is behind the main body of emigrants, but can of course easily overtake them. He expresses much anxiety for their safe journey, and is determined to do all in his power to assist them, a promise of much value, as well from his practical good sense as his general knowledge of the route.[42]

Whitman was accompanied by a nephew, Perrin. They set off in the wake of the emigrant caravan with no other food than a boiled ham; Whitman expected the emigrants to feed him, which they did.

Peter Burnett recounted an early confrontation with an Indian war party, on 6 June:

On the 6th we met a war party of Kansas and Osage Indians, numbering about ninety warriors. They were all mounted on horses, and their faces painted red, and had with them one Pawnee scalp, with the ears to it, and with the wampum in them. One of them, who spoke English well, said they had fasted three days, and were very hungry. Our guide, Captain Gant, advised us to furnish them with provisions; otherwise, they would steal some of our cattle. We deemed this not only good advice but good humanity, and furnished these starving warriors with enough provisions to satisfy their hunger. They had only killed one Pawnee, but had divided the scalp, making several pieces, some with the ears on, and part with the cheek. Two of this party were wounded, one in the shoulder and the other in some other part of the body.

None of us knew anything about a trip across the Plains, except our pilot Captain Gant, who had made several trips with small parties of hired and therefore disciplined men, who knew how to obey orders. But my company was composed of very different materials; and our pilot had no knowledge that qualified him to give me sound advice. I adopted rules and endeavored to enforce them, but found much practical difficulty and opposition; all of which I at first attributed to the fact that our emigrants were green at the beginning, but comforted myself with the belief that they would improve in due time; but my observation soon satisfied me that matters would grow worse. It became very doubtful whether so large a body of emigrants could be practically kept together on such a journey. These considerations induced me to resign on the 8th of June, and William Martin was elected as my sucessor.[10]

Two men who jointly composed a memoir of the 1843 migration here describe the awe they felt on first reaching open prairie, inhabited only by Indians:

After leaving the country of the Shawnees we came next into that of the Kanzas Indians. Theirs, also, is a very beautiful country; entirely in a state of nature. If differs but little from the Western part of Missouri, except that the surface is more undulating, and that it has less timber. Here we left the last traces of civilization, and seemed, for a time, to be beyond even the borders of animated existence. Not even the song of a bird broke upon the surrounding stillness; and, save the single track of the Emigrants, winding away over the hills, not a footprint broke the rich, unvaried verdure of the broad forest-begirt prairies; and in the little islet groves that dotted the plain – the wooded strips that wound along with the course of the rivulet – and the blue wall that surrounded, not a trunk was scarred nor a twig was broken. It was a vast, beautiful and perfect picture, which nature herself had drawn, and the hand of man had never violated. . . . [23]

Jessie A. Applegate, then a small boy, had vivid memories of the animals of the prairie, especially how an antelope out-ran one of his father's greyhounds. Jesse's father was Lindsay Applegate, brother of another Jesse Applegate, who was with the 'Cow Column'.

The prairie dogs seemed to prefer city life, for we always found them living in towns and cities. The population of some of their cities I should think was as great as that of Greater New York. The dog is about the size of a very young puppy dog. As we would pass through or near their towns they would come up out of their holes and sit up straight on their hind quarters, always near their burrow, and utter something like a yelp, or so it seemed to me, and on the slightest alarm drop into their holes. I saw owls sitting among them, and it was said that prairie dogs, owls, and rattlesnakes lived together in the same holes. . . .

Antelope and long-eared rabbits were everywhere. Father had two black dogs called greyhounds; they were very fast runners and could soon pick up a rabbit, but when they chased an antelope it was quite different. One day an antelope had in some way been separated from the herd and ran through the train. One of the dogs, Fleet by name, pursued the antelope, and the chase led across a level plain. The black dog as he sped on with all his might, looked like a crane flying along the plain. We were all excited, for the dog was gaining on the antelope at every bound and would no doubt soon overtake him. The dog thought so too, for when he was within a few yards of the antelope and expected in another bound or two to seize its prey, he gave a yelp, but that yelp seems to have been a fatal mistake, for that antelope, in a few seconds after that bark, was fifty yards away from the dog and flying over the plain as if he had been shot out of a gun. He actually passed over many yards before we could see the dust rise behind him. The dog was so astounded that he stopped short, and after gazing at the antelope for a moment, no doubt amazed beyond expression, turned about and trotted back to the train. It was said that dog would never chase an antelope afterwards.[2]

Peter Burnett told of the initial adjustment men had to make to trail conditions:

A trip to Oregon with ox teams was at that time a new experiment, and was exceedingly severe upon the temper and endurance of people. . . . At the beginning of the journey there were several fisticuff fights in camp; but the emigrants soon abandoned that practice, and thereafter confined themselves to abuse in words only. The man with a black eye and battered face could not well hunt up his cattle or drive his team. . . .

Our emigrants were placed in a new and trying position, and it was interesting to see the influence of pride and old habits over men. They were often racing with their teams in the early portion of the journey, though they had before them some seventeen hundred miles of travel. No act could have been more inconsiderate than for men, under such circumstances, to injure their teams simply to gratify their ambition. Yet the proper rule in such a case was to allow any and every one to pass you who desired to do so. Our emigrants, on the first portion of the trip, were about as wasteful of their provisions as if they had been at home. When portions of bread were left over, they were thrown away; and, when any one came to their tents, he was invited to eat. I remember well that, for a long time, the five young men I had with me refused to eat any part of the bacon rind, which accordingly fell to my share, in addition to an equal division of the bacon. Finally they asked for and obtained their portion of the bacon rind, their delicate appetites having become ravenous on the trip. Those who were in the habit of inviting every one to eat who stood around at meal-times, ultimately found that they were feeding a set of loafers and gave up the practice.[10]

Several travellers on the trails wrote with affection of their ox teams, and praised their endurance and dependability.

Burnett:

We could see our faithful oxen dying inch by inch, every day becoming weaker, and some of them giving out, and left in the wilderness to fall a prey to the wolves. In one or two instances they fell dead under the yoke, before they would yield. We found, upon a conclusive trial, that the ox was the noblest of draft-animals upon that trip, and possessed more genuine hardihood and pluck than either mules or horses. When an ox is once broken down, there is no hope of saving him. It requires immense hardship, however, to bring him to that point. He not only gathers his food more rapidly than the horse or mule, but he will climb rocky hills, cross muddy streams, and plunge into swamps and thickets for pasture. He will seek his food in places where other animals will not go. On such a trip as ours one becomes greatly attached to his oxen, for upon them his safety depends.[10]

Burnett describes the wagon train's arrival at the Platte River and the journey along its valley:

Ever since we crossed Kansas River we had been traveling up Blue River, a tributary of the former. On the 17th of June we reached our last encampment on Blue. We here saw a band of Pawnee Indians, returning from a buffalo-hunt. They had quantities of dried buffalo-meat, of which they generously gave us a good supply. They were fine-looking Indians, who did not shave their heads, but cut their hair short like white men.

On the 18th of June we crossed from the Blue to the great Platte River, making a journey of from twenty-five to thirty miles, about the greatest distance we ever traveled in a single day. The road was splendid, and we drove some distance into the Platte bottom, and encamped in the open prairie without fuel. Next morning we left very early, without breakfast, having traveled two hundred and seventy-one miles from the rendezvous, according to the estimated distance recorded in my journal.

We traveled up the south bank of the Platte, which, at the point where we struck it, was from a mile to a mile and a half wide. Though not so remarkable as the famed and mysterious Nile . . . the Platte is still a remarkable stream. Like the Nile, it runs hundreds of miles through a desert without receiving any tributaries. Its general course is almost as straight as a direct line. It runs through a formation of sand of equal consistence; and this is the reason its course is so direct.

The valley of the Platte is about twenty miles wide, through the middle of which this wide, shallow, and muddy stream makes its rapid course. Its banks are low, not exceeding five or six feet in height; and the river bottoms on each side seemed to the eye a dead level, covered with luxuriant grass. Ten miles from the river you come to the foot of the table-lands, which are also apparently a level sandy plain, elevated some hundred and fifty feet above the river bottoms. On these plains grows the short buffalo-grass, upon which the animal feeds during a portion of the year. As the dry season approaches, the water, which stands in pools on these table-lands, dries up, and the buffaloes are compelled to go to the Platte for water to drink. They start for water about 10 A.M., and always travel in single file, one after the other, and in parallel lines about twenty yards apart, and go in a direct line to the river. They invariably travel the same routes over and over again, until they make a path some ten inches deep and twelve inches wide. These buffalo-paths constituted quite an obstruction to our wagons, which were heavily laden at this point in our journey. Several axles were broken. We had been apprised of the danger in advance, and each wagon was supplied with an extra axle.

In making our monotonous journey up the smooth valley of the Platte, through the warm genial sunshine of summer, the feeling of drowsiness was so great that it was extremely difficult to keep awake during the day. Instances occurred where the drivers went to sleep on the road, sitting in the front of their wagons; and the oxen, being about as sleepy, would stop until the drivers were aroused from their slumber. My small wagon was only used for the family to ride in; and Mrs. Burnett and myself drove and slept alternately during the day.

One great difficulty on this part of the trip was the scarcity of fuel. Sometimes we found dry willows, sometimes we picked up pieces of drift-wood along the way, which we put into our wagons, and hauled them along until we needed them. At many points of the route up the Platte we had to use buffalo-chips. By cutting a trench some ten inches deep, six inches wide, and two feet long, we were enabled to get along with very little fuel. At one or two places the wind was so severe that we were forced to use the trenches in order to make a fire at all.[10]

A picture that stayed in young Jesse A. Applegate's mind was how fire was started without matches.

I remember that to get fire at times a man would rub a cotton rag in powder and shoot it out of a musket, or put it in the pan of a flint-lock gun, and then explode the powder in the pan; often a flint steel and punk were used. . . .[2]

This stage of the journey, along the Platte, was the setting for a short classic of its kind, Jesse Applegate's A Day with the Cow Column.

The presence of upwards of five thousand head of cattle had soon

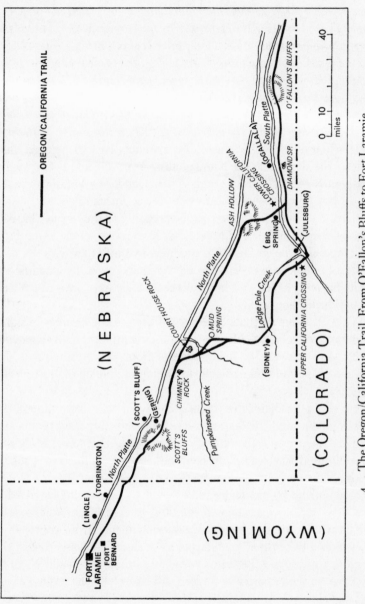

— OREGON/CALIFORNIA TRAIL

(NEBRASKA)

(WYOMING)

(COLORADO)

FORT LARAMIE
FORT BERNARD

(LINGLE)
(TORRINGTON)

North Platte

(SCOTT'S BLUFF)
(GERING)

SCOTT'S BLUFFS

CHIMNEY ROCK

Pumpkinseed Creek

COURT HOUSE ROCK

North Platte

MUD SPRING

ASH HOLLOW

Lodge Pole Creek

(SIDNEY)

UPPER CALIFORNIA CROSSING

LOWER CALIFORNIA

(OGALLALA)
CROSSING

South Platte

BIG SPRING

(JULESBURG)

DIAMOND SP.

O'FALLON'S BLUFFS

0   10   40
miles

4.   The Oregon/California Trail. From O'Fallon's Bluffs to Fort Laramie

become cause for dissension. Emigrants without cattle were not prepared to help guard or drive the herds, nor to adjust their pace to that of the slower moving animals. Therefore, after crossing the Big Blue River, the emigrants divided into two main groups, the cattle group, which fell behind, being known as the Cow Column. Jesse Applegate, a thirty-two-years-old Kentuckian, was chosen head of the Cow Column. He had been deputy of the surveyor-general's office in St Louis. One of the reasons that caused him to join the migration of 1843 was a dislike of slavery.

It is four o'clock a.m.; the sentinels on duty have discharged their rifles – the signal that the hours of sleep are over; and every wagon and tent is pouring forth its night tenants, and slow-kindling smokes begin largely to rise and float away on the morning air.

Sixty men start from the corral, spreading as they make through the vast herd of cattle and horses that form a semi-circle around the encampment, the most distant perhaps two miles away.

The herders pass to the extreme verge and carefully examine for trails beyond, to see that none of the animals have strayed or been stolen during the night.

This morning no trails lead beyond the outside animals in sight, and by five o'clock the herders begin to contract the great moving circle and the well-trained animals more slowly toward camp, clipping here and there a thistle or a tempting bunch of grass on the way.

In about an hour five thousand animals are close up to the encampment, and the teamsters are busy selecting their teams and driving them inside the 'corral' to be yoked. The corral is a circle one hundred yards deep, formed with wagons connected strongly with each other, the wagon in the rear being connected with the wagon in front by its tongue and ox chains. It is a strong barrier that the most vicious ox cannot break, and in case of an attack of the Sioux would be no contemptible entrenchment. From six to seven o'clock is a busy time; breakfast is to be eaten, the tents struck, the wagons loaded, and the teams yoked and brought in readiness to be attached to their respective wagons. All know when at seven o'clock, the signal to march sounds, that those not ready to take their proper places in the line of march must fall into the dusty rear for the day.

There are sixty wagons. They have been divided into fifteen divisions or platoons of four wagons each, and each platoon is entitled to lead in its turn. The leading platoon of today will be the rear one tomorrow, and will bring up the rear unless some teamster, through indolence or negligence, has lost his place in the line, and is con-condemned to that uncomfortable post. It is within ten minutes of seven; the corral but now a strong barricade is everywhere broken, the teams being attached to the wagons. The women and children have taken their places in them. The pilot (a borderer who has passed his life on the verge of civilization, and has been chosen to the post of leader from his knowledge of the savage and his experience in travel through roadless wastes) stands ready in the midst of his pioneers, and aids to mount and lead the way. . . .

It is on the stroke of seven; the rushing to and fro, the cracking of the whips, the loud command to oxen, and what seems to be the inextricable confusion of the last ten minutes has ceased. Fortunately every one has been found and every teamster is at his post. The clear notes of the trumpet sound in the front; the pilot and his guards mount their horses, the leading division of wagons moves out of the encampment, and takes up the line of march, the rest fall into their places with the precision of clock work, until the spot so lately full of life sinks back into that solitude that seems to reign over the broad plain and rushing river as the caravan draws its lazy length toward the distant El Dorado. . . .

The caravan has been about two hours in motion and is now extended as widely as is prudent for safety to permit. First near the bank of the shining river, is a company of horsemen; they seem to have found an obstruction, for the main body has halted while three or four ride rapidly along the bank of the creek or slough. They are hunting a favorable crossing for the wagons . . . it has apparently required no work to make it passable, for all but one of the party have passed on and he has raised a flag, no doubt a signal to the wagons to steer their course to where he stands. The leading teamster sees him though he is yet two miles off, and steers his course directly towards him, all the wagons following in his track. They (the wagons) form a line three quarters of a mile in length; some of the teamsters ride upon the front of their wagons, some walk beside their teams; scattered along the line companies of women and children are taking exercise on foot; they gather bouquets of rare and beautiful flowers that line the way; near them stalks a stately gray hound or an Irish wolf dog, apparently proud of keeping watch and ward over his master's wife and children.

Next comes a band of horses; two or three men or boys follow them, the docile and sagacious animals scarce needing this attention, for they have learned to follow in the rear of the wagons, and know that at noon they will be allowed to graze and rest, their knowledge of time seems as accurate as of the place they are to occupy in the line, and even a full bloom thistle will scarcely tempt them to straggle or halt until the dinner hour has arrived – not so with the large herd of horned beasts that bring up the rear; lazy, selfish and unsocial, it has been a task to get them in motion, the strong always ready to domineer over the weak, halt in the front and forbid the weaker to pass them. They seem to move only in fear of the driver's whip; though in the morning full to repletion, they have not been driven an hour before their hunger and thirst seem to indicate a fast of days' duration.

Through all the long day their greed is never sated nor their thirst quenched, nor is there a moment of relaxation of the tedious and vexatious labors of their drivers, though to all the others the march furnishes some season of relaxation and enjoyment. For the cow-drivers there is none. . . .

The pilot, by measuring the ground and timing the speed of the wagons and the walk of his horse, has determined the rate of each, so as to enable him to select the nooning place, as nearly as the requisite grass and water can be had at the end of five hours' travel of the wagons. Today the ground being favorable, little time has been lost in preparing the road, so that he and his pioneers are at the nooning place an hour in advance of the wagons, which time is spent in preparing convenient watering places for the animals and digging little wells near the bank of the Platte. As the teams are not unyoked, but simply turned loose from the wagons, a corral is not formed at noon, but the wagons are drawn up in columns, four abreast, the leading wagon of each platoon on the left, – the platoon being formed with that in view. This brings friends together at noon as well as at night.

Today an extra session of the council is being held, to settle a dispute that does not admit of delay, between a proprietor and a young man who has undertaken to do a man's service on the journey for board and bed. Many such engagements exist and much interest is taken in the manner this high court, from which there is no appeal, will define the right of each party in such engagements. The council was a high court in the most exalted sense. It was a Senate composed of the ablest and most respected fathers of the emigration. It exercised both legislative and judicial powers, and its laws and decisions proved it equal and worthy of the high trust reposed in it. Its session were usually held on days when the caravan was not moving. It first took the state of the little commonwealth into consideration; revised or repealed rules defective or obsolete, and exacted such others as exigencies seemed to require. The commonwealth being cared for, it next resolved itself into a court, to hear and settle private disputes and grievances. The offender and aggrieved appeared before it, witnesses were examined, and the parties were heard by themselves and sometimes by counsel. The judges thus being made fully acquainted with the case, and being in no way influenced or cramped by technicalities, decided all cases according to their merits. There was but little use for lawyers before this court, for no plea was entertained which was calculated to defeat the ends of justice. Many of these judges have since won honors in higher spheres. They have aided to establish on the broad basis of right and universal liberty two of the pillars of our great Republic in the Occident. Some of the young men who appeared before them as advocates have themselves sat upon the highest judicial tribunals, commanded armies, been Governors of States, and taken high positions in the Senate of the nation.

It is now one o'clock; the bugle has sounded, and the caravan has resumed its westward journey. It is in the same order, but the evening is far less animated than the morning march; a drowsiness has fallen apparently on man and beast; teamsters drop asleep on their perches and even walking by their teams, and the words of command are now addressed to the slowly creeping oxen in the softened tenor of women or the piping treble of children, while the snores of themselves make a droning accompaniment.

But a little incident breaks the monotony of the march. An emigrant's wife whose state of health has caused Dr. Whitman to travel near the wagon for the day, is now taken with violent illness, the doctor has had the wagon driven out of the line, a tent pitched and a fire kindled. Many conjectures are hazarded in regard to this mysterious proceeding, and as to why this last wagon is to be left behind.

And we must leave it, hasten to the front and note the proceedings, for the sun is now getting low in the west, and at length the painstaking pilot is standing ready to conduct the train in a circle which he has previously measured and marked out, which is to form the invariable fortification for the night. The leading wagons follow him so nearly round the circle, that but a wagon length separates them. Each wagon follows in its track; the rear closing on the front, until its tongue and ox chains will perfectly reach from one to the other, and so accurate the measurement and perfect the practice, that the hindmost wagon of the train always precisely closes the gateway, as each wagon is brought into position. It is dropped from its team, (the teams being inside into position), the team unyoked, and the yokes and chains are used to connect the wagon strongly with that in its front. Within ten minutes from the time the leading wagon halted, the barricade is formed, the teams unyoked and driven out to pasture.

Everyone is busy preparing fires of buffalo chips to cook the evening meal, pitching tents and otherwise preparing for the night. There are anxious watches for the absent wagon, for there are many matrons who may be afflicted like its inmate before the journey is over; and they fear the strange and startling practice of the Oregon doctor will be dangerous. But as the sun goes down, the absent wagon rolls into camp, the bright, speaking face and cheery look of the doctor, who rides in advance, declares without words that all is well, and both mother and child are comfortable. I would fain now and here pay a passing tribute to that noble, devoted man, Dr. Whitman. . . .

From the time he joined us on the Platte until he left us at Fort Hall, his great experience and indomitable energy were of priceless value to the migrating column. His constant advice, which we knew was based upon a knowledge of the road before us, was – 'travel, travel, travel – nothing else will take you to the end of your journey; nothing is wise that does not help you along. Nothing is good for you that causes a moment's delay.' He was a great authority as a physician and complete success in the case above referred to saved us many prolonged and perhaps ruinous delays from similar causes, and it is no disparagement to others to say, that to no other individual are the emigrants of 1843 so much indebted for the successful conclusion of their journey as to Dr. Whitman.

All able to bear arms in the party have been formed into three companies, and each of these into four watches. Every third night it is the duty of one of these companies to keep watch and ward over the camp, and it is so arranged that each watch takes its turn of guard duty through the different watches of the night. . . .

It is not eight o'clock when the first watch is to be set; the evening meal is just over, and the corral now free from the intrusion of the cattle or horses, groups of children are scattering over it. The larger are taking a game of romps, 'the wee toddling things' are being taught that great achievement that distinguishes man from the lower animals. Before a tent near the river a violin makes lively music, and some youths and maidens have improvised a dance upon the green; in another quarter a flute gives its mellow and melancholy notes to the still air, which as they float away over the quiet river seem a lament for the past rather than a hope for the future. It has been a prosperous day; more than twenty miles have been accomplished of the great journey. The encampment is a good one; one of the causes that threaten much future delay has just been removed by the skill and energy of 'that good angel', Dr. Whitman, and it has lifted a load from the hearts of the elders. Many of these are assembled around the good Doctor at the tent of the pilot (which is his home for the time being), and are giving grave attention to his wise and energetic counsel. The careworn pilot sits aloof, quietly smoking his pipe, for he knows the brave doctor is 'strengthening his hands'.

But time passes; the watch is set for the night, the council of old men has broken up and each has turned to his own quarter. The flute has whispered its last lament to the deepening night, the violin is silent and the dancers have dispersed. Enamored youths have whispered a tender 'good night' in the ears of blushing maidens, or stolen a kiss from the lips of some future bride – for Cupid here as elsewhere has been busy bringing together congenial hearts, and among those simple people he alone is consulted in forming the marriage ties. Even the Doctor and the pilot have finished their confidential interview and have separated for the night. All is hushed and repose from the fatigue of the day, save the vigilant guard, and the wakeful leader who still has cares upon his mind that forbid sleep.[1]

Peter Burnett, on the South Fork crossing:

On the 29th of June we arrived at a grove of timber, on the south bank of the South Fork of the Platte. This was the only timber we we had seen since we struck the river, except on the islands, which were covered with cottonwoods and willows. From our first camp upon the Platte to this point, we had traveled, according to my estimates recorded in my journal, one hundred and seventy-three miles, in eleven days.

On July 1st we made three boats by covering our wagon-boxes or beds with green buffalo-hides sewed together, stretched tightly over the boxes, flesh side out, and tacked on with large tacks; and the boxes, thus covered, were then turned up to the sun until the hides were thoroughly dry. This process of drying the green hides had to be repeated several times. From July 1st to the 5th, inclusive, we were engaged in crossing the river.[10]

In fording where the water was running fast and deep, wagons sometimes overturned or sank, and animals, and occasionally people, drowned. Jesse A. Applegate recalled a small boy's excitement at the Platte crossings:

I remember crossing two Platte rivers. One crossing where we forded, the river seemed to be very wide and quite rapid; the water was so deep in places that it ran into the wagon boxes and a single team wagon would have been swept away, so they formed the entire train in single file, and attached the teams and wagons to a chain extending through the entire length of the train. The crossing here severely tried the courage and endurance of the men, for they waded the river alongside their oxen, at times clinging to the ox yokes, and swimming; at some deep places the teams seemed to swim and the wagons to float, being held up and in line by the chain to which they were attached.

Whether at this crossing or another, I do not remember, but at one place where we forded one of the rivers, mother, myself, and the other children were in a wagon, which we called 'the little red wagon'; it was drawn by one yoke of oxen, and it appears to me now that our wagon was attached to the last end of the train. As we were just getting up the bank from the ford our team broke loose and wagon and team backed into the river. Being swept below the ford, the team swam and the wagon sank down, and was drifting on the sand; and I remember the water came rushing into the wagon box to my waist, compelling me to scramble up on to the top of a trunk or something of the kind. But several men came to our assistance immediately, and, swimming, held up the wagon, and soon assisted us to the shore. Probably this was at the fording of the North Platte.[2]

In camp at the South Fork crossing, James W. Nesmith, then aged twenty-three, who became one of Oregon's leading citizens and a Senator, wrote in his diary:

Saturday, July 1. – Some stir in camp this morning in consequence of a sentinel's gun going off accidentally, which killed a mule belonging to James Williams, the bullet breaking the mule's neck. This is the most serious accident which has yet occurred from carelessness in the use of fire-arms, though, judging from the carelessness of the men, I have anticipated more serious accidents before this time, and if they do not occur, they will be avoided by great good luck, not by precaution. In the afternoon the company crossed several loads in wagon bodies, which they have covered with raw buffalo hides to prevent their leaking. Captain Applegate and Dr. Whitman came into camp this evening, their company being camped eight miles below this place. Mr. Stewart had the gratification of being presented with a daughter this evening. Weather cool and pleasant.

Tuesday, July 4. – The glorious Fourth has once more rolled around. Myself, with most of our company, celebrated it by swimming and fording the south fork of the Big Platte, with cattle, wagons, baggage and so forth. All this at Sleepy Grove. However, there seems to be some of our company ruminating upon luxuries destroyed in different parts of the great Republic on this day. Occasionally you hear something said about mint julips, soda, ice cream, cognac, porter, ale and sherry wine, but the Oregon emigrant must forget these luxuries and, for a time, submit to hard fare, and put up with truly cold-water celebrations, such as we have enjoyed today, namely, drinking cold water, and wading and swimming in it all day. . . .[34]

On 14 July the emigrants reached the fur-trading post of Fort Laramie, which had an Indian encampment near by. Here the caravan stayed two days, trading and repairing wagons. They had travelled well over six hundred miles.

Burnett:

At the Fort we found the Cheyenne chief and some of his people. He was a tall, trim, noble-looking Indian, aged about thirty. The Cheyennes at that time boasted that they had never shed the blood of the white man. He went alone very freely among our people, and I happened to meet him at one of our camps, where there was a foolish, rash young man, who wantonly insulted the chief. Though the chief did not understand the insulting words, he clearly comprehended the insulting tone and gestures. I saw from the expression of his countenance that the chief was most indignant, though perfectly cool and brave. He made no reply in words, but walked away slowly; and, when some twenty feet from the man who had insulted him, he turned around, and solemnly and slowly shook the forefinger of his right hand at the young man several times, as much as to say, 'I will attend to your case.'

I saw there was trouble coming, and I followed the chief, and by kind earnest gestures made him understand at last that this young man was considered by us all as a half-witted fool, unworthy of the notice of any sensible man; . . . The moment the chief comprehended my meaning I saw a change come over his countenance, and he went away perfectly satisfied. . . .

In traveling up the South Fork we saw several Indians, who kept at a distance, and never manifested any disposition to molest us in any way. They saw we were mere travelers through their country, and would only destroy a small amount of their game. Besides, they must have been impressed with a due sense of our power. Our long line of wagons, teams, cattle, and men, on the smooth plains, and under the clear skies of Platte, made a most grand appearance. They had never before seen any spectacle like it. They, no doubt, supposed we had cannon concealed in our wagons. A few years before a military expedition had been sent out from Fort Leavenworth to chastize some of the wild prairie tribes for depredations committed against the whites. General Bennet Riley, then Captain Riley, had command, and had with him some cannon. In a skirmish with the Indians, in the open prairie, he had used his cannon, killing some of the Indians at a distance beyond rifle-shot. This new experience had taught them a genuine dread of big guns.

The Indians always considered the wild game as much their property as they did the country in which it was found. Though breeding and maintaining the game cost them no labor, yet it lived and fattened on their grass and herbage, and was as substantially within the power of these roving people and skillful hunters as the domestic animals of the white man.[10]

By 7 August they were through the South Pass, and had crossed from the Atlantic to the Pacific watershed, a heady moment, though one difficult to locate on so gradual a gradient.

James Nesmith had stopped to inscribe his name, and that of some girls, on Independence Rock.

Most beautiful morning, the weather calm and serene. After breakfast, myself, with some other young men, had the pleasure of waiting on five or six young ladies to pay a visit to Independence Rock. I had the satisfaction of putting the names of Miss Mary Zachary and Miss Jane Mills on the southeast point of the rock, near the road, on a high point. Facing the road, in all the splendor of gunpowder, tar and buffalo grease, may be seen the name of J. W.

Nesmith, from Maine, with an anchor. Above it on the rock may be found the names of trappers, emigrants, and gentlemen of amusement, some of which have been written these ten years. . . .[34]

Matthew Field, returning in September with the gentlemen's hunting party saw evidence of the emigrants' passage on the trail from near the South Pass to Fort Laramie, and reported in the New Orleans Daily Picayune, *21 November 1843:*

We found the now-deeply-worn road strewn with indications of their recent presence. Scaffolds for drying meat, broken utensils thrown away, chips showing where wagons had been repaired, and remnants of children's shoes, frocks, etc., met our notice at every encampment.

But one death seemed to have occurred among them, and this was far out under the mountains. Here the loose riders of our moving camp gathered one morning to examine a rude pyramid of stones by the roadside. The stones had been planted firmly in the earth, and those on top were substantially placed, so that the wolves, whose marks were evident about the pile, had not been able to disinter the dead. On one stone, larger than the rest, and with a flat side, was rudely engraved:

J. Hembree

and we place it here, as perhaps the only memento those who knew him in the States may ever receive of him. How he died we cannot of course surmise, but there he sleeps among the rocks of the West, as soundly as though chiseled marble was built above his bones.[18]

The occupant of the grave was a child killed in an accident. Dr Marcus Whitman wrote to a friend on 20 July, from Big Butte Creek: 'We buried a small boy this morning that died from a wagon having passed over the abdomen.'

Field was impressed to learn of the fast progress the emigrants had made on the trail.

On returning to Rock Independence, a point about nine hundred miles from the settlements, we were astonished at finding that the Oregonians had reached and passed it only four days behind us.

We had confidently supposed them fully four weeks in our rear, and their rapid progress argues well for the success of their enterprise. On the rock we found printed:

THE OREGON CO.

arrived

July 26, 1843.

At Fort Laramie we were told that they were still well provisioned when passing there, and could even afford to trade away flour, coffee, etc., for necessaries of other kinds. But it was droll to hear how the Sioux stared at the great caravan. Some of them on seeing the great number of wagons, and particularly white women and children, for the first time, began to think of coming down here, having seen, as they supposed, *the whole white village* move up beyond the mountains.[18]

On the 9th [*Burnett resumes*] we came to the Big Sandy at noon. This day Stevenson died of fever, and we buried him on the sterile banks of that stream. On the 11th we crossed Green River, so called from its green color. It is a beautiful stream, containing fine fish. On the margins of this stream there are extensive groves of small cottonwood-trees, about nine inches in diameter, with low and brushy tops. These trees are cut down by the hunters and trappers in winter, for the support of their mules and hardy Indian ponies. The animals feed on the tender twigs, and on the bark of the smaller limbs, and in this way manage to live. Large quantities of this timber are thus destroyed annually.

On the 12th of August we were informed that Dr. Whitman had written a letter, stating that the Catholic missionaries had discovered, by the aid of their Flathead Indian pilot, a pass through the mountains by way of Fort Bridger, which was shorter than the old route. We therefore determined to go by the fort. There was a heavy frost with thin ice this morning. On the 14th we arrived at Fort Bridger, situated on Black's Fork of Green River, having traveled from our first camp on the Sweetwater two hundred and nineteen miles in eighteen days. Here we overtook the missionaries. On the 17th we arrived on the banks of Bear River, a clear, beautiful stream, with abundance of good fish and plenty of wild ducks and geese. On the 22nd we arrived at the great Soda Springs, . . .[10]

Here J. C. Frémont and his party were camped. An interesting encounter for the boy Jesse.

We camped very near one of these springs and nearly a quarter of a mile from Bear River, a rapid stream about the width of Green River. Here we met Frémont, with his party, and I thought their large tent, which was spread near our encampment, a very nice affair. There was a soda spring or pool between the camps, and Frémont's men were having a high time drinking soda water. They were so noisy that I suspected they had liquor stronger than soda mixed with the water. Frémont had a cannon, the first I had ever seen, a six-pounder, they said, and made of bright shining brass. It was resting on a low carriage, which was standing between our camp and Frémont's, and near the soda spring. I admired this cannon very much and examined it very closely several times. I discovered a touch hole near the breech and, looking in at the muzzle, could see the ball, or thought I could. After Frémont's men had been drinking soda water from that spring, and enjoying it greatly nearly a whole day, one of our company fished out an enormous frog from the pool, almost as large as a young papoose, and falling to pieces with rottenness. Soon after this discovery we noticed that the hilarity at the Frémont tent suddenly ceased. I thought Frémont was a very fine looking young man. In fact, all his party were pretty well dressed, and jolly fellows. . . .[2]

The emigrants now left Bear River for Fort Hall, established as a fur-trading post by Nathaniel Wyeth in 1834 (the same year that Forts Laramie and Boise were constructed) and sold by him to the Hudson's Bay Company two years later. The advance of the 1843 migration reached the fort on 27 August. There fur-traders advised the travellers to leave their wagons and cattle and complete the journey on horseback. Hitherto this had been the practice. In 1836, Marcus Whitman, in his notable crossing with his wife and the Spaldings, had taken a wagon as far as Fort Boise, but a wagon metamorphosed into a cart, using the back two wheels, and putting the front two wheels and a broken axle-tree on to the cart. And in 1840 fur-trappers Joseph Meek, Robert

Newell, and Caleb Wilkins had taken the bare chassis of three wagons abandoned at Fort Hall through the Blue Mountains to the Columbia River, to be told by Whitman: 'You have broken the ice, and when others see that wagons haved passed, they, too, will pass, and in a few years the valley will be full of our people.' But complete, loaded wagons were another matter, and travellers in '41 and '42, if they did not abandon their wagons at Fort Laramie, did so at Fort Hall. All the advice from the traders there was to do so.

Perrin Whitman overheard Captain Richard Grant, in charge at Fort Hall, advising the emigrants of '43 to sell their wagons and cattle, and carried this information to his uncle. Dr Whitman gathered the travellers together and told them forcefully that in his opinion wagons could be taken through to the Columbia River and down the turbulent waters on rafts or bateaux to the Willamette Valley. He convinced most of the party, and was hired to be pilot for the remainder of the journey, a purse of four hundred dollars being raised. He went ahead with a small party with light wagons. The others followed, in several groups. A few emigrants changed from wagons to pack mules, but the majority started their wagons rolling again towards Oregon, under the spell of Whitman's conviction, yet anticipating that anxious and difficult days lay ahead. Burnett describes their mood:

We had now arrived at a most critical period in our most adventurous journey; and we had many misgivings as to our ultimate success in making our way with our wagons, teams, and families. We had yet to accomplish the untried and most difficult portion of our long and exhaustive journey. We could not anticipate at what moment we might be compelled to abandon our wagons in the mountains, pack our scant supplies upon our poor oxen, and make our way on foot through this terribly rough country, as best we could. . . . Dr. Whitman assured us that we could succeed, and encouraged and aided us with every means in his power. . . .

On the 30th of August we quitted Fort Hall, many of our young men having left us with pack-trains. Our route lay down Snake River for some distance. The road was rocky and rough, except in the dry valleys; and these were covered with a thick growth of sage or wormwood, which was from two to three feet high, and offered a

great obstruction to the first five or six wagons passing through it.
The soil where this melancholy shrub was found appeared to be too
dry and sterile to produce anything else. It was very soft on the
surface, and easily worked up into a most disagreeable dust, as fine
as ashes or flour . . .

On the 7th of September, 1843, we arrived at the Salmon Falls on
Snake River . . . .[10]

Jesse A. Applegate:

We were now approaching the Salmon Falls in Snake River, and
heard the roar of the waters a long time before we saw them. The
first sound that struck my ear seemed to jar the earth like distant
thunder. As we approached, many Indians were seen, and long
lines of something of a red color, which I thought were clothes hung
out to dry, attracted my attention; but as we came nearer I learned
that those lines were salmon which the Indians were drying in the
sun. The company made a halt here, whether for noon or over night,
I don't remember. Many Indians visited our camp, bringing fish,
both fresh and dried, which they exchanged for old clothes, and a
number of them strutted around dressed in their newly acquired gar-
ments, seeming to enjoy their often absurd appearance as much as we
did, for when we would laugh, they would laugh and jabber among
themselves. They were almost naked, some of them quite so. When
one would get a garment he would put it on at once. A naked Indian
would put on a shirt and step around as though he thought himself
in full dress; another would seem delighted with nothing but a vest;
another big buck with only a hat on would grin and seem as pleased
as if he were 'dressed to kill'. This was grand sport for us children,
and the Indians did not seem to object to our fun at their expense.
The fish which the Indians brought no doubt were very acceptable
to the emigrants, as I do not remember having any before, except at
Bear River, where the men caught an abundance of very large trout.[2]

*In crossing the Snake River, an emigrant, Miles Eyres, was drowned.
He carried all his money in a belt around his waist, and his body was not
recovered. His almost destitute wife and children were cared for through
the following winter at the mission at Waiilatpu, a service extended
to other emigrants until the Whitmans were killed by Indians in 1847.*

James Nesmith joined Jesse Applegate, Peter Burnett, and other chroniclers, in praising Whitman:

While with us he was clad entirely in buckskin, and rode one of those patient long-eared animals said to be 'without pride of ancestry or hope of posterity'. The Doctor spent much of his time in hunting out the best route for the wagons, and would plunge into streams in search of practical fords, regardless of the depth or temperature of the water, and sometimes after the fatigue of a hard day's march, would spend much of the night in going from one part to another to minister to the sick.³⁴

Burnett:

On the 14th of September we passed the Boiling Spring. Its water is hot enough to cook an egg. . . . On the 20th of September we arrived at Fort Boise. . . . On the 21st we recrossed the Snake River by fording, which was deep but safe. On the 24th we reached Burnt River, so named from the many fires that have occurred there, destroying considerable portions of timber. . . . On the 27th of September we had some rain during the night, and next morning left Burnt River. To-day we saw many of the most beautiful objects in nature. In our rear, on our right and left, were ranges of tall mountains, covered on the sides with magnificent forests of pine, the mountain-tops being dressed in a robe of pure snow; and around their summits the dense masses of black clouds wreathed themselves in fanciful shapes, the sun glancing through the open spaces upon the gleaming mountains. We passed through some most beautiful valleys, and encamped on a branch of the Powder River, at the Lone Pine.

This noble tree stood in the centre of a most lovely valley, about ten miles from any other timber. . . .

On the 29th and 30th of September we passed through rich, beautiful valleys, between ranges of snow-clad mountains, whose sides were covered with noble pine forests. On October 1st we came into and through Grande Ronde, one of the most beautiful valleys in the world, embosomed among the Blue Mountains, which are covered with magnificent pines. It was estimated to be about a hundred miles in circumference. It was generally rich prairie, covered with luxuriant grass, and having numerous beautiful streams passing through it, most of which rise from springs at the foot of the mountains bordering the valley. In this valley the camas-root abounds, which the Indians dried upon hot rocks. We purchased some from them, and found it quite palatable to our keen appetites.

On the 2nd of October we ascended the mountain-ridge at the Grande Ronde, and descended on the other side of the ridge to a creek, where we camped. These hills were terrible.[10]

Jesse A. Applegate had vivid memories of a stretch of the trail called the Devil's Backbone:

We had to follow the 'Devil's Backbone', and it may have been a mile or more; it is a very narrow ridge with a gorge a thousand feet deep on the left hand and a sheer precipice on the right down to Snake River, which looked as though it might be a mile or more away. Indeed, it was so far away that it looked like a ribbon not more than four inches wide. The danger was so great that no one rode in the wagons. As I walked behind a wagon I would often look into the gorge on the left and then down to the river on the right, and as I remember it now, at many places there was not a foot to spare for the wagon wheels between the bottomless gorge on the left and the precipice down to the river on the right. . . . But we passed it in safety, and again were slowly tramping over a broad and level expanse of sage brush and greasewood.[2]

Young Jesse fell off a wagon and a front wheel passed over the small of his back and a hind wheel over his legs. He luckily escaped serious injury.

At the Grande Ronde, east of the Blue Mountains, Whitman received word that Henry Spalding and his wife were critically ill with scarlet fever and believed they were dying. Whitman left the piloting of the emigrants to one of his converts, a Cayuse chief called Stickus, and hurried to Lapwai, where he found that the Spaldings were making a fast recovery to health. He stayed one night, then rode to his own mission station, anxious to make preparations for the arrival of the emigrants. He reached the station at the end of September to find that an advance party of the emigrants had already arrived, breaking into the mission house to hunt for food, and leaving it open to the Indians. Meanwhile, the bulk of the emigrants, piloted by Stickus, were crossing the Blue Mountains. They reached the vicinity of Whitman's mission on 10 October.

Burnett acquitted Dr Whitman of the unjust charge of profiteering from the sales of flour and potatoes, pointing out that some of the new arrivals had not appreciated that the prices of these provisions were higher in Oregon than in the western states they had set out from five months before.

Peter Burnett arrived at Fort Walla Walla on 16 October. The total journey from the rendezvous near Independence he estimated at 1,691 miles, covered between 22 May and 16 October, an average of eleven and a half miles per day. He concludes:

A portion of our emigrants left their wagons and cattle at Walla Walla, and descended the Columbia in boats; while another, and the larger portion, made their way with their wagons and teams to the Dalles, whence they descended to the Cascades on rafts, and thence to Fort Vancouver in boats and canoes.[10]

Frémont's Second Expedition reached the Walla Walla River, on 23 October. Frémont reported:

In six miles we crossed a principal fork, below which the scattered water of the river was gathered into one channel; and, passing on the way several unfinished houses, and some cleared patches, where corn and potatoes were cultivated, we reached, in about eight miles farther, the missionary establishment of Dr. Whitman, which consisted, at this time, of one *adobe* house – *i.e.*, built of unburnt bricks, as in Mexico.

I found Dr. Whitman absent on a visit to the *Dalles* of the Columbia; but had the pleasure to see a fine-looking large family of emigrants, men, women, and children, in robust health, all indemnifying themselves for previous scanty fare in a hearty consumption of potatoes, which are produced here of a remarkably good quality. . . .

A small town of Nez Percé Indians gave an inhabited and even a populous appearance to the station; and after remaining about an hour, we continued our route, and encamped on the river about four miles below, passing on the way an emigrant encampment. . . .[19]

Frémont moved on to Fort Walla Walla (sometimes called Nez Percé) . . .

... one of the trading establishments of the Hudson's Bay Company, a few hundred yards above the junction of the Walahwalah with the Columbia river. Here we had the first view of this river, and found it about 1,200 yards wide, and presenting the appearance of a fine navigable stream. . . . [19]

The river is, indeed, a noble object, and has here attained its full magnitude. About nine miles above, and in sight from the heights about the post, is the junction of the two great forks which constitute the main stream – that on which we had been travelling from Fort Hall, and known by the names of Lewis's fork, Shoshonee, and Snake river; and the North fork, which has retained the name of Columbia, as being the main stream.

We did not go up to the junction, being pressed for time; but the union of two large streams, coming one from the southeast and the other from the northeast, and meeting in what may be treated as the geographical centre of the Oregon valley, thence doubling the volume of water to the ocean, while opening two great lines of communication with the interior continent, constitutes a feature in the map of the country which cannot be overlooked; and it was probably in reference to this junction of waters, and these lines of communication, that this post was established. They are important lines, and, from the structure of the country, must for ever remain so – one of them leading to the South Pass, and to the valley of the Mississippi; the other to the pass at the head of the Athabasca river, and to the countries drained by the waters of the Hudson Bay. The British fur companies now use both lines; the Americans, in their emigration to Oregon, have begun to follow the one which leads towards the United States. . . . To the emigrants to Oregon, the Nez Percé is a point of interest, as being, to those who choose it, the termination of their overland journey. The broad expanse of the river here invites them to embark on its bosom; and the lofty trees of the forest furnish the means of doing so.

From the South Pass to this place is about 1,000 miles; and as it is about the same distance from that pass to the Missouri river at the mouth of the Kansas, it may be assumed that 2,000 miles is the *necessary* land travel in crossing from the United States to the

Pacific Ocean on this line. . . . At the time of our arrival, a considerable body of the emigrants under the direction of Mr. Applegate, a man of considerable resolution and energy, had nearly completed the building of a number of Mackinaw boats, in which they proposed to contine their further voyage down the Columbia. I had seen, in descending the Walahwalah river, a fine drove of several hundred cattle, which they had exchanged for California cattle, to be received at Vancouver, and which are considered a very inferior breed. The other portion of the emigration had preferred to complete their journey by land along the banks of the Columbia, taking their stock and wagons with them. . . .[19]

Frémont's party, with horses and provisions, resumed their journey down the left bank of the Columbia.

The country to-day was very unprepossessing, and our road bad; and as we toiled slowly along through deep loose sands, and over fragments of black volcanic rock, our laborious travelling was strongly contrasted with the rapid progress of Mr. Applegate's fleet of boats, which suddenly came gliding swiftly down the broad river, which here chanced to be tranquil and smooth. . . .[19]

Later, on the Dalles of the Columbia, a boat capsized and two Applegate children, and a man, were drowned.

Jesse A. Applegate:

During the time we remained at Walla Walla, probably two weeks, the men were busy sawing lumber and building small boats. They called them skiffs, and one of average size would carry a family of eight or ten persons. The lumber was sawed by hand with a pitsaw, from timber that had drifted to that place when the river was very high. To carry out the plan of descending the Columbia River to the Willamette country in those small boats, it was of course, necessary to leave the wagons and cattle behind. The cattle and horses were branded with the Hudson Bay Company's brand, 'H.B.', and the property was understood to be under the protection of that company.[2]

The swift passage by boat down the river was a memorable experience for young Jesse.

Shoving out from the Walla Walla canoe landing about the first of November, our little fleet of boats began the voyage down the great 'River of the West'. Whirlpools looking like deep basins in the river, lapping, splashing, and rolling of waves, crested with foam sometimes when the wind was strong, alarmed me for a day or two on the start. But I soon recovered from this childish fear, and as I learned that the motion of the boat became more lively and gyratory, rocking from side to side, leaping from wave to wave, or sliding down into a trough and then mounting with perfect ease to the crest of a wave, dashing the spray into our faces when we were in rough water, the sound of rapids and the sight of foam and white caps ahead occasioned only pleasant anticipation. Often when the current was strong, the men would rest on their oars and allow the boats to be swept along by the current.[2]

But the rapids led to a disaster for one of the other boats. Jesse continues:

We had an Indian pilot, probably selected by McKinley [*in charge*] at Fort Walla Walla, although I do not positively remember noticing the pilot before we entered the rapids we were now approaching. At the head of those rapids the river bears from a west course a little northerly, making a very gradual curve. As we approached this bend I could hear the sound of rapids, and presently the boat began to rise and fall and rock from side to side. When we began to make the turn I could see breakers ahead extending in broken lines across the river, and the boat began to sweep along at a rapid rate. The pilot squatted low in the bow. An old red handkerchief was tied around his head and his long black hair hung down his back. There were now breakers on the right and on the left, and occasionally foam-crested waves swept across our bows. The motion of the boat had never been so excitingly delightful before – it was an exaggeration of the cradle and grape vine swing combined. I began to think this was no ordinary rapid, but felt reassured when I noticed that the older people sat quietly in their places and betrayed no sign of fear. Rocked on the heaving bosom of the great river and lulled by the medley of sounds, the two babies had fallen asleep in their mother's arms. Our boat now was about twenty yards from the right-hand shore; when looking across the river I saw a smaller boat about opposite to us near the

south bank. The persons in this boat were Alexander McClellan, a
man about seventy years old, William Parker, probably twenty-one,
and William Doke, about the same age, and three boys: Elisha Applegate, aged about eleven, and Warren and Edward Applegate, each
about nine years old. This boat now near the south shore, it would
seem, should have followed our boat as the pilot was with us, and this
was a dangerous part of the river. But there was little time to consider
mistakes or to be troubled about what might be the consequences,
for presently there was a wail of anguish, a shriek, and a scene of
confusion in our boat that no language can describe. The boat we
were watching disappeared and we saw the men and boys struggling
in the water. Father and Uncle Jesse, seeing their children drowning,
were seized with frenzy, and dropping their oars, sprang up from
their seats and were about to leap from the boat to make a desperate
attempt to swim to them, when mother and Aunt Cynthia, in voices
that were distinctly heard above the roar of the rushing waters, by
commands and entreaties brought them to a realization of our own
perilous situation, and the madness of an attempt to reach the other
side of the river by swimming. . . .[2]

*William Doke was hauled into a passing boat. William Parker and
Elisha Applegate (a brother of Jesse) swam to an island and then
followed a narrow causeway of rock to the main land. But Warren
Applegate was swept away and never seen again, and the old man,
McClellan, died trying, in vain, to save the life of Edward Applegate.
Both boys drowned were sons of Jesse Applegate.*

*Because of its size and importance the 1843 movement to Oregon
was called 'The Great Emigration'. Whitman estimated it as being two
hundred families, and about one thousand people. As could be said of the
crossing in 1841 to California, a number of these pioneers were to become
leading citizens of the country they settled in. James W. Nesmith became
Senator for Oregon. Peter H. Burnett moved south and became the
first Governor of the State of California. Jesse Applegate explored safer
routes into Oregon and played a prominent part in the development of
Oregon as both Territory and State. But there was a tragic end for
Dr Marcus Whitman. Immigrants in 1847 carried an epidemic of
measles that killed half the Cayuse Indians. There was a tribal custom*

*that a medicine man who failed could be killed; in addition, Indians
began to suspect that the mysterious deaths in their ranks were due to
white men poisoning Indians to get their lands. On 29 November 1847,
Cayuses slaughtered Marcus Whitman, his wife, and twelve of his
workers, at the Waiilatpu mission. Two children, ill with measles, died
from neglect. Five men, eight women, and thirty-four children were held
captive by Indians until ransomed for clothing, ammunition, blankets,
and tobacco worth five hundred dollars. The Indians fled when a volun-
teer force from the Willamette Valley moved against them.*

*But at least Whitman had seen his hopes realized with regard to
Oregon. He had written on 16 May 1844 to his wife's parents:*

As I hold the settlement of this country by Americans rather than
by an English colony most important, I am happy to have been the
means of landing so large an emigration on to the shores of the
Columbia, with their wagons, families and stock, all in safety.[44]

*Settlers of the Willamette, growing tired of no positive response from
Washington to their petitions for American jurisdiction, set up their own
provisional government, a constitution being adopted at a mass meeting
on 5 July 1843. Every settler was allowed 640 acres of land.*

*During the very wet spring of 1844 three parties set out for Oregon
from the eastern frontier, variously estimated between 700 and 1,500
people. Accounts of the '44 crossing are few. One company, led by John
Thorp, followed the north bank of the Platte, to be taken by the Mormons
in '47 and '48. Heavy rains made river crossings hazardous in '44,
and many animals and some people were drowned.*

*Wagon trains in 1845 took an estimated three thousand people to
Oregon. The largest caravan was led by mountain man Stephen Meek.
He said he knew a short cut through desert to the southern end of the
Willamette Valley. Oxen dropped dead in large numbers, and twenty
people perished before a rescue party could reach them. Meek was
lucky not to be lynched by irate emigrants.*

*In 1846 the United States and Great Britain reached agreement over the
Oregon territory. The northwest as far as the 49th parallel was to become
American territory. The presence of so many American settlers had been
the decisive factor. And the key crossing had been 'The Great Emigration'
of 1843, which had shown that wagon trains could get through.*

Disaster in the Mountains:
The Donner Party,
1846

No wagon trains set out for California in 1842; but that year Joseph B. Chiles, of the Bidwell crossing of '41, mqde the return trip east and in the following spring led west a party of emigrants that included four women and five small children. Chiles took with him some mill machinery which he hoped could be put into profitable operation in California. As in '41, they set out a little west of Independence. On the trail Chiles met Joseph Reddeford Walker, an experienced mountain man and pioneer pathfinder. At Fort Hall the emigrants split into two groups. A party of thirteen of the younger men, including Chiles, followed the Oregon route as far as Fort Boise, from which they swung south-west to follow the Sacramento River into northern California. Meanwhile, Walker took the wagons, the women and children, and the older men, south along the Humboldt River, skirted the eastern foothills of the Sierra Nevada, and entered southern California early in December through Walker Pass – a route pioneered by Walker in 1834. They had abandoned the wagons and the mill machinery on 20November at Owens Lake, east of the Sierras.

The only overland party to California in 1844 set out before learning of the failure in '43 to take wagons through. It was composed mostly of families: twenty-three men, eighteen women, and fifteen children. Elisha Stevens, a blacksmith, was the elected captain, though the party is sometimes named after Martin Murphy (whose Irish tribe made up half the company) or Dr John Townsend, a farmer-physician. Old mountain man Caleb Greenwood went with them as guide. Some of the party, along with the wagons, were snowed up in the Sierras – they had tackled the centre of the range at Truckee Pass. One woman gave birth in the mountains. The wagons were finally taken through in the spring of 1845. It was a notable achievement.

Thereafter there was regular annual spring and summer traffic west on the California Trail, culminating in the fantastic gold rush of 1849.

In 1845, at Fort Hall, old Caleb Greenwood persuaded two hundred *and fifty emigrants, with fifty wagons, to dismiss Oregon from their minds and take the now open California Trail. For a fee of 125 dollars Caleb led the party in the tracks of the Stevens Party and successfully reached Sutter's Fort in mid-October. Overland migration was now established fact. Little Sarah Ide could remember the crossing of '45 to California as '* a "pleasure-trip" – so many beautiful wild flowers, such wild scenery, mountains, rocks, and streams – something at every turn'. *But that was a child's view, buoyant because free from the weight of responsibilities. Events in 1846 were to prove that taking wagons to California was no picnic outing.*

Publication of reports of overland crossings west made in 1844 and word of the successful journeys of 1845 stimulated interest in emigration to the Pacific coastal regions. In '45 fifty wagons had been taken by Caleb Greenwood into the Sacramento Valley – in '46 two hundred were made ready to go. Another sign of growing confidence in emigration to California was the number of professional men – lawyers, physicians, clergymen, schoolteachers – who joined with farmers and tradesmen and their families in making up the company. The party even included a former governor of Missouri, Lilburn W. Boggs.

Unless one travelled as a hired hand of some kind, a measure of wealth was required to equip for the journey. A family needed at least one covered wagon, three yoke of oxen to pull it, and provisions to last five to six months' arduous travel. Some of the wagons in '46 were large and luxurious, the most splendid of all being that of James F. Reed, a wealthy manufacturer of furniture, of Scotch-Irish blood.

Reed and his wife and four children were with a group of emigrants from Springfield, Illinois, which in the same year elected Abraham Lincoln to Congress. Prominent Springfield families opting for a new life in California were those of the brothers Donner, George and Jacob, well-to-do farmers, of German ancestry. When the great caravan split up into smaller groups, a customary feature of trail travel, George Donner gave his name to a party which essayed the untried Hastings's cut-off, fell behind, and was caught in snow blizzards in the Sierras. The Donner Party disaster was the worst to befall any emigrant train to California. Forty of the party's eighty-seven people died, and some survived only by resorting to eating the flesh of dead companions.

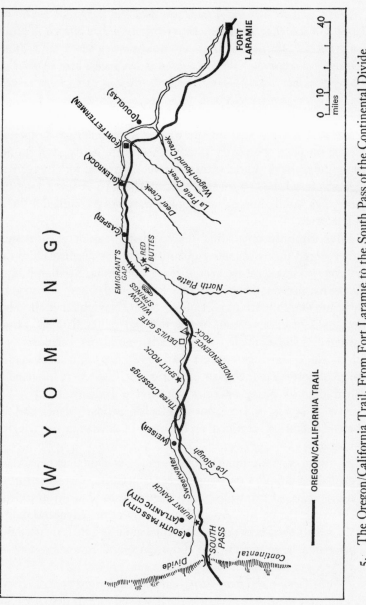

(W Y O M I N G)

FORT LARAMIE

(FORT FETTERMAN)

(DOUGLAS)

(GLENROCK)

(CASPER)

RED BUTTES

EMIGRANT'S GAP

WILLOW SPRINGS

DEVIL'S GATE

SPLIT ROCK

INDEPENDENCE ROCK

Three Crossings

(WEISER)

SOUTH PASS CITY (ATLANTIC CITY)

BURNT RANCH

SOUTH PASS

Continental Divide

Wagon Hound Creek

La Prele Creek

Deer Creek

North Platte

Ice Slough

Sweetwater

OREGON/CALIFORNIA TRAIL

0   10   40
miles

5.   The Oregon/California Trail. From Fort Laramie to the South Pass of the Continental Divide

George Donner was one of those who died that winter, as did his wife Tamsen, a schoolteacher with literary talents and an interest in botany. Unfortunately the journal of the overland journey which she kept with a view to publication, like her botanical specimens, was never found. However, Eliza, one of George Donner's five daughters, later wrote an account of the journey. She tells of the practical preparations for such a venture:

Strong, commodious emigrant wagons were constructed especially for the purpose. The oxen to draw them were hardy, well trained, and rapid walkers. Three extra yoke were provided for emergencies. Cows were selected to furnish milk on the way. A few young beef cattle, five saddle-horses, and a good watch-dog completed the list of live stock.

After carefully calculating the requisite amount of provisions, father stored in his wagons a quantity that was deemed more than sufficient to last until we should reach California. Seed and implements for use on the prospective farms in the new country also constituted an important part of our outfit. Nor was that all. There were bolts of cheap cotton prints, red and yellow flannels, bright-bordered handkerchiefs, glass beads, necklaces, chains, brass finger rings, earrings, pocket looking-glasses, and divers other knickknacks dear to the hearts of aborigines. These were intended for distribution as peace offerings among the Indians. Lastly, there were rich stores of laces, muslins, silks, satins, velvets and like cherished fabrics, destined to be used in exchange for Mexican land-grants . . .

A liberal sum of money for meeting incidental expenses and replenishing supplies on the journey, if need be, was stored in the compartments of two wide buckskin girdles, to be worn in concealment about the person. An additional sum of ten thousand dollars, cash, was stitched between the folds of a quilt for safe transportation. This was a large amount for those days, and few knew that my parents were carrying it with them. . . .[22]

For the Donner children, setting out was an exciting event:

Thursday, April 15, 1846, was the day fixed for our departure, and the members of our household were at work before the rosy dawn.

We children were dressed early in our new linsey travelling suits; and as the final packing progressed, we often peeped out of the window at the three big white covered wagons that stood in our yard.

In the first were stored the merchandise and articles not to be handled until they should reach their destination; in the second, provisions, clothing, camp tools, and other necessaries of camp life. The third was our family home on wheels, with feed boxes attached to the back of the wagon-bed for Fanny and Margaret, the favourite saddle-horses, which were to be kept ever close at hand for emergencies.

Early in the day, the first two wagons started, each drawn by three yoke of powerful oxen, whose great moist eyes looked as though they too had parting tears to shed. The loose cattle quickly followed, but it was well on towards noon before the family wagon was ready.[22]

Farewells were said, then the family wagon moved off.

I sat beside my mother with my hand clasped in hers, as we slowly moved away from that quaint old house on its grassy knoll, from the orchard, the corn land, and the meadow; as we passed through the last pair of bars, her clasp tightened, and I, glancing up, saw tears in her eyes and sorrow in her face. I was grieved at her pain, and in sympathy nestled closer to her side and sat so quiet that I soon fell asleep.[22]

The Donner family reached Independence, Missouri, on 11 May ...

... with our wagons and cattle in prime condition, and our people in the best of spirits. Our party encamped near that bustling frontier town, and were soon a part of the busy crowds, making ready for the great prairie on the morrow. Teams thronged the highways; troops of men, women, and children hurried nervously about seeking information and replenishing supplies. Jobbers on the street were crying their wares, anxious to sell anything or everything required, from a shoestring to a complete outfit for a four months' journey across the plains. Beads of sweat clung to the merchants' faces as they rushed to and fro, filling orders. Brawny blacksmiths, with breasts bared and sleeves rolled high, hammered and twisted red hot metal into the divers forms necessary to repair yokes and wagons.

Good fellowship prevailed as strangers met, each anxious to learn something of those who might by chance become his neighbors in line.[22]

On the move again, Eliza was impressed by the sight of the great 'prairie schooners' coming from Sante Fé to Independence for merchandise.

We could hear them from afar, for the great wagons were drawn by four or five span of travel-worn horses or mules, and above the hames of each poor beast was an arch hung with from three to five clear-toned bells, which jingled merrily as their carriers moved along, guided by a happy-go-lucky driver, usually singing or whistling a gleeful tune. Both man and beast looked longingly towards the town, which promised companionship and revelry to the one, and rest and fodder to the other.

We overtook similar wagons, heavily laden with goods bound for Sante Fé.[22]

They averaged a distance oj about two and a half miles per hour, and camped at nights where fuel and water could be obtained. Early on 19 May they reached the main camp at Soldiers' Creek, a tributary of the Kansas River. Edwin Bryant who had been editor of the Louisville Courier, *was at the camp, and wrote in his journal:*

May 19, 1846. A new census of our party was taken this morning, and it was found to consist oi 98 fighting-men, 50 women, 46 wagons, and 350 cattle. Two divisions were made of the wagons, for convenience in marching. We were joined to-day by nine wagons from Illinois, beloning to Mr. Reed and the Messrs. Donner, highly respectable and intelligent gentlemen, with interesting families. They were received into the company by a unanimous vote.[9]

Eliza tells us of the varied nature of these eager pioneers:

... lawyers, journalists, teachers, students, farmers, and day-laborers, also a minister of the gospel, a carriage-maker, a cabinet-maker, a stonemason, a jeweller, a blacksmith, and women versed in all branches of woman's work.[22]

The government of such emigrant trains was ...

... essentially democratic and characteristically American. A captain was chosen, and all plans of action and rules and regulations were proposed at a general assembly, and accepted or rejected by majority vote.[22]

The captain elected in this case was 'Colonel' William Henry Russell, a former U.S. marshal, nicknamed 'Owl'.

In the early days of the journey the roads were heavy and there were frequent spring storms, but these alternated with 'intervening hours of calm and sunshine'. *Eliza Donner describes the relatively care-free beginnings of a journey that was to end in disaster:*

The staid and elderly matrons spent most of their time in their wagons, knitting or patching designs for quilts. The younger ones and the girls passed theirs in the saddle. They would scatter in groups over the plains to investigate distant objects, then race back, and with song and banter join husband and brother, driving the loose cattle in the rear. The wild, free spirit of the plain often prompted them to invite us little ones to seats behind them, and away we would canter with the breeze playing through our hair and giving a ruddy glow to our cheeks.[22]

In return for gifts, Indians escorted the train for part of the way. A raft had to be constructed to cross the Big Blue, which had become swollen and turbulent after the heavy rains.

Eliza:

Bright and early . . . boat-builders went to work with a will, and by the close of day had felled two trees about three and a half feet in diameter, had hollowed out the trunks, and made of them a pair of canoes twenty-five feet in length. In addition to this, they had also prepared timbers for the frames to hold them parallel, and insure the wagon wheels a steady place while being ferried across the river. . . .

The craft being finished on the morning of the thirtieth of May, was christened *Blue Rover*, and launched amid cheers of the company. Though not a thing of beauty, she was destined to fulfil the expectations of our worthy Captain. One set of guide-ropes held her in place at the point of embarkation, while swimmers on horseback carried another set of ropes across the river and quickly made them fast. Only one wagon at a time could cross, and great difficulty was experienced in getting the vehicles on and off the boat. Those working near the bank stood in water up to their armpits, and frequently were in grave peril. By the time the ninth wagon was safely landed, darkness fell. . . .

Much anxiety was experienced when the cattle were forced into the water . . . Each family embarked in its own wagon, and the last was ferried over in the rain at nine o'clock that night. The ropes were then detached from the *Blue Rover*, and she drifted away in the darkness.[22]

On 2 June, Edwin Bryant wrote in his journal:

It was proposed, in order to relieve ourselves from the consequences of disputes in which we had no interest, that all the Oregon emigrants should, in a respectful manner and a friendly spirit, be requested to separate themselves from the California emigrants, and start on in advance of us. The proposition was unanimously carried, and the spirit in which it was made prevented any bad feeling, which otherwise might have resulted from it. The Oregon emigrants immediately drew their wagons from the *corral* and proceeded on their way.[9]

Eliza Donner:

The Oregon company was never so far in advance that we could not hear from it, and on various occasions, some of its members sent to us for medicines and other necessaries.

Our fear of the Pawnees diminished as we proceeded, and met in their haunts only friendly Indians returning from the hunt, with ponies heavily laden with packs of jerked meats and dried buffalo tongues. At least one brave in each party could make himself understood by word or sign. Many could pronounce the one word 'hogmeat', and would show what they had to exchange for the coveted luxury. Others also begged for 'tobac', and sugar, and generally got a little.

A surprising number of trappers and traders, returning to the United States with their stocks of peltry, camped near us from time to time. They were glad to exchange information, and kept us posted in regard to the condition of the migrants, and the number of wagons on the road in advance. . . .

Another means of keeping in touch with traveling parties in advance was the accounts that were frequently found written on the

1. Wagon train west

2. John Bidwell in 1850

3. Independence, Missouri, in the eighteen-forties. By Edmund Flagg

4. Ferrying across the North Platte. By Charles Nahl

5. (*top left*) Chimney Rock. Sketch by Father Pierre Jean de Smet
6. (*bottom left*) Fort Laramie in 1842. From a contemporary sketch
7. (*above*) Soda Springs. Sketched by Father Pierre Jean de Smet

St. Clair Co. mo.
April 11th 1843

Dear Brother.

I will start with my family to the Oregon Ty. this Spring — Lindsay and perhaps Charles go with me. This resolution has been conceived and matured in a very short time. but it is probably destiny. to which account I place it having neither time nor good reasons to offer in defence of so wild an undertaking — We are all well and I only snatch this opportunity to write to you for the purpose of ascertaining if the same Species of madness exists on your side of the Mo.

If you are going to Oregon by all means go this Spring for if Linn's Bill pass next year every man and every man's neighbors and friends will moove in that direction. —

Write immidiately and meet us if possible at the rendezvous. armed and equipt as the journey requires —

Your affectionate Brother
Jesse Applegate

8. (*top left*) Peter Hardeman Burnett in 1849
9. (*bottom left*) Jesse A. Applegate
10. (*above*) Letter written by Jesse Applegate to his brother Lisbon, shortly before joining the 'Cow Column', 1843

11. Wagon train crossing sage plain in Snake River Valley.
By Major Osborne Cross, 1849

12. Outer and inner views of Fort Hall.
Drawn by Major Osborne Cross, 1849

13. Descent after leaving the Blue Mountains.
By Major Osborne Cross, 1849

14. Whitman's Mission at Waiilatpu in 1843

15. Remains of wagons abandoned in the salt desert by the
Donner Party in 1846. In the foreground, the bones of an ox

16. Fort Sutter. From an engraving, *c.* 1848

17. (*top left*) Brigham Young in 1850. From a daguerrotype
18. (*bottom left*) William Clayton, appointed historian for the Mormons' trek
to Salt Lake Valley

19. (*top*) Mormon emigrant train
20. (*below*) Salt Lake City in 1853. From a contemporary engraving

21. Gold mining in California

22. Illustration from Alonzo Delano's *Life on the Plains*.
Depicts an incident in the fight with Indians described on page 162

23. 'The Overland Route.' From Alonzo Delano's *Life on the Plains*

bleaching skulls of animals, or on trunks of trees from which the
bark had been stripped, or yet again, on pieces of paper stuck in the
clefts of sticks driven into the ground close to the trail. Thus each
company left greetings and words of cheer to those who were
following. Lost cattle were also advertised by that means, and many
strays or convalescents were found and driven forward to their
owners.[22]

*By the middle of June the conditions for travel had become more
difficult. Eliza continues:*

We entered a region of oppressive heat. Clouds of dust enveloped
the train. Wood became scarce, and water had to be stored in casks
and carried between supply points. We passed many dead oxen, also
a number of poor cripples that had been abandoned by their
unfeeling owners. Our people, heeding these warnings, gave our
cattle extra care, and lost but few.[22]

*But by now the Donners could anticipate brief rest and relaxation
at Fort Laramie, a few more days ahead on the trail.*

*On the Oregon Trail in '46 was a young Bostonian not long out of
Harvard College. Despite the title of his classic,* The California and
Oregon Trail, *Francis Parkman's interest was not in emigration or
emigrants, but in Indians. He and a young companion has set out on
horseback from St Joseph. They reached Fort Laramie ahead of a large
caravan and were given the fort's best apartment. Historian Parkman
was intrigued by Fort Laramie, which resembled one of the extinct
eighteenth-century French trading posts:*

Fort Laramie is one of the posts established by the 'American Fur
Company', who well-nigh monopolize the Indian trade of this whole
region. Here its officials rule with an absolute sway; the arm of the
United States has little force; for when we were there, the extreme
outposts of her troops were about seven hundred miles to the eastward. The little fort is built of bricks dried in the sun, and externally
is of an oblong form, with bastions of clay, in the form of ordinary
blockhouses, at two of the corners. The walls are about fifteen feet
high, and surmounted by a slender palisade. The roofs of the
apartments within, which are built close against the walls, serve the
purpose of a banquette.

D

Within, the fort is divided by a partition; on one side is the square area, surrounded by the store-rooms, offices, and apartments of the inmates; on the other is the *corral*, a narrow place, encompassed by the high clay walls, where at night, or in presence of dangerous Indians, the horses and mules of the fort are crowded for safe keeping. The main entrance has two gates, with an arched passage intervening. A little square window, quite high above the ground, opens laterally from an adjoining chamber into this passage; so that when the inner gate is closed and barred, a person without may still hold communication with those within, through this narrow aperture. This obviates the necessity of admitting suspicious Indians, for purposes of trading, into the body of the fort; for when danger is apprehended, the inner gate is shut fast, and all traffic is carried on by means of the little window. . . . [36]

Near Fort Laramie was a Dakota village, in which Parkman was to spend many evenings. But his first sight of its Indians was when they appeared en masse *at the fort, in expectation of drinking coffee and eating biscuits with each emigrant party shortly to arrive from the east. A disorderly swarm of savages, on horseback and on foot, came over the hills beyond Laramie Creek, descended to the water and began to cross.*

The stream is wide, and was then between three and four feet deep, with a very swift current. For several rods the water was alive with dogs, horses, and Indians. The long poles used in pitching the lodges are carried by the horses, being fastened by the heavier end, two or three on each side, to a rude sort of pack-saddle, while the other end drags on the ground. About a foot behind the horse, a kind of large basket or pannier is suspended between the poles, and firmly lashed in its place. On the back of the horse are piled various articles of luggage; the basket also is well filled with domestic utensils, or, quite as often, with a litter of puppies, a brood of small children, or a superannuated old man. Numbers of these curious vehicles, called in the bastard language of the country, *travaux*, were now splashing together through the stream. Among them swam countless dogs, often burdened with miniature *travaux*; and dashing forward on horseback through the throng came the superbly-formed warriors, the slender figure of some lynx-eyed boy clinging fast behind them. The women sat perched on the pack-saddles, adding not a little to the load of the already overburdened horses. The confusion was prodigious. The dogs yelled and howled in chorus; the puppies in the *travaux* set up a dismal whine as the water invaded their comfortable retreat; the little black-eyed children, from one year of age upward, clung fast with both hands to the edge of their basket, and looked over in alarm at the water rushing so near them, sputtering and making wry mouths as it splashed against their faces. Some of the dogs, encumbered by their load, were carried down by the current, yelping piteously; and the old squaws would rush into the water, seize their favourites by the neck, and drag them out. As each horse gained the bank, he scrambled up as he could. Stray horses and colts came among the rest, often breaking away at full speed through the crowd, followed by the old hags, screaming, after their fashion, on all occasions of excitement. Buxom young squaws, blooming in all the charms of vermilion, stood here and there on the bank, holding aloft their master's lance, as a signal to collect the scattered portions of the household.

In a few moments the crowd melted away; each family, with its horses and equipage, filing off to the plain at the rear of the fort; and here, in the space of half an hour, arose sixty or seventy of their tapering lodges. Their horses were feeding by hundreds over the surrounding prairie, and their dogs were roaming everywhere. The fort was full of men, and the children were whooping and yelling incessantly under the walls.[36]

Shortly afterwards . . .

. . . the heavy caravan of the emigrant wagons could be seen, steadily advancing from the hills. They gained the river, and, without turning or pausing, plunged in; they passed through, and slowly ascending the opposing bank, kept directly on their way by the fort and the Indian village, until, gaining a spot a quarter of a mile distant, they wheeled into a circle.

For some time our tranquility was undisturbed. The emigrants were preparing their encampment; but no sooner was this accomplished, than Fort Laramie was fairly taken by storm. A crowd of broad-brimmed hats, thin visages, and staring eyes, appeared suddenly at the gate. Tall awkward men, in brown home-spun; women with cadaverous faces and long lank figures, came thronging in together, and, as if inspired by the very demon of curiosity, ransacked every nook and corner of the fort. . . .

Having at length satisfied their curiosity, they next proceeded to business. The men occupied themselves in procuring supplies for their onward journey; either buying them with money, or giving in exchange superfluous articles of their own.

The emigrants felt a violent prejudice against the French Indians, as they called the trappers and traders. They thought, and with some justice, that these men bore them no good will. Many of them were firmly persuaded that the French were instigating the Indians to attack and cut them off.[36]

Parkman visited the emigrants' encampment, and was . . .

. . . at once struck with the extraordinary perplexity and indecision that prevailed among the emigrants. They seemed like men totally out of their element; bewildered and amazed, like a troop of school-boys lost in the woods. It was impossible to be long among them without being conscious of the bold spirit with which most of them were animated. But the *forest* is the home of the backwoodsman. On the remote prairie he is totally at a loss. He differs as much from the genuine 'mountain-man' . . . as a Canadian voyageur, paddling his canoe on the rapids of the Ottawa, differs from an American sailor among the storms of Cape Horn[36].

As hundreds of emigrants – their trains split by dissensions and con-flicting interests into many small units – were moving westward, a group of men, which included Lansford W. Hastings, author of The Emi-grants' Guide to Oregon and California, *had come eastward from California on horseback, with the purpose of meeting the emigrants and offering their services as guides. James Clyman, an experienced mountain man, went ahead to Fort Laramie. In his diary he told of his first sight of the emigrant wagon trains of '46.*

[June] 23   Early on our saddles and in about 3 hours we met the advance company of oregon Emigration consisting of Eleven wagons nearly oposite the red Butes   when we came in sight of N. Platte we had the Pleasant sight of Beholding the valy to a greate distance dotted with Peopl Horses cattle wagons and Tents . . .

24 Down the N. Platte and during the day we passed three small companies some for Oregon and some for california

It is remarkable how anxious thes people are to hear from the Pacific country and strange that so many of all kinds and classes of People should sell out comfortable homes in Missouri and Elsewhare pack up and start across such an emmence [*immense*] Barren waste to settle in some new Place of which they have at most so uncertain information but this is the character of my countrymen

25 . . . To day we met all most one continual stream of Emigrants wending their long and Tedious march to oregon & california . . .

26 . . . met 117 teams in six different squads all bound for oregon and california . . .

27 we met numerous squad of emigrants untill we reached fort Larimie whare we met Ex govornor Boggs and party from Jackson county Mi[ss]ourie Bound for California and we camped with them several of us continued the conversation untill a late hour.[14]

The nature of the prolonged conversation was revealed by Clyman years later :

We met Gov. Boggs and party at Fort Laramie. [*Boggs had superseded Russell as Captain*] It included the Donner Party. We camped one night with them at Laramie. . . . Mr. Reed . . . was enquiring about the route. I told him to 'take the regular wagon track [*by way of Fort Hall*] and never leave it – it is barely possible to get through if you follow it – and it may be impossible if you dont.' Reed replied, 'There is a nigher route, and it is of no use to take so much of a roundabout course.' I admitted the fact, but told him about the great desert and the roughness of the Sierras, and that a straight route might turn out to be impracticable.

The party when we separated took my trail by which I had come from California, south of Salt Lake, and struck the regular emigrant trail again on the Humboldt.[14]

The Reed/Donner party made their decision on 20 July, by vote of the men, after leaving Fort Laramie and reaching Little Sandy River. There

some Oregon emigrants were resting their cattle preparatory to entering upon the dry drive of forty miles known as Greenwood's Cut-off, and later as Sublette's Cut-off, which took one on to the Fort Bridger to Fort Hall trail. The alternative was to travel south-west to Fort Bridger. There emigrants for California could still decide whether to take the route via Fort Hall, or the new cut-off south of Great Salt Lake. The Reed/Donner party had already made their decision.

They were led to do so [*Eliza Donner tells us*] by 'An Open Letter', which had been delivered to our company on the seventeenth by special messenger on horseback. The letter was written by Lansford W. Hastings. . . . It was dated and addressed: 'At the Headwaters of the Sweetwater: To all California Emigrants now on the Road', and . . . urged those on the way to California to concentrate their numbers and strength, and take the new and better route which he had explored from Fort Bridger, by way of the south end of Salt Lake. It emphasized the statement that this new route was nearly two hundred miles shorter than the old one by way of Fort Hall and the headwaters of Ogden's River, and that he himself would remain at Fort Bridger to give further information, and to conduct the emigrants through to the settlement.

The proposition seemed so feasible, that after cool deliberation and discussion, a party was formed to take the new route.

My father was elected captain of this company, and from that time on it was known as the 'Donner Party'.[22]

At least one member of the party was uneasy about the decision. J. Q. Thornton, one of the travellers who followed the old route, recorded in his journal:

The Californians were much elated and in fine spirits, with the prospect of a better and much nearer road to the country of their destination. Mrs. George Donner, however, was an exception. She was gloomy, sad, and dispirited in view of the fact that her husband and others could think of leaving the old road, and confide in the statement of a man of whom they knew nothing, but was probably some selfish adventurer.[43]

The clarion prose of the letter to the people on the trail was characteristic of the man John Bidwell called 'a political adventurer'. Lansford

Warren Hastings, a young lawyer from Ohio, had made the overland journey to Oregon in '42, moving shortly afterwards to California. In '44 he travelled across Mexico, before spending the winter of that year in Missouri giving lectures on the evils of intemperance in order to raise money to publish a book. In The Emigrants' Guide to Oregon and California, *which came out in '45, Hastings eulogized California as a country ripe for settlement:*

In my opinion, there is no country in the known world possessing a soil so fertile and productive, with such varied and inexhaustible resources, and a climate of such mildness, uniformity, and salubrity; nor is there a country now known which is so eminently calculated by nature herself in all respects to promote the unbounded prosperity of civilised and enlightened man.[21]

Edwin Bryant – who, at Fort Laramie, with some young bachelor friends, had changed from wagons to pack mules – arrived at Fort Bridger on 20 July. First train to arrive was the advance of the Young/Harlan party, of about 160 people, whom Hastings talked into taking the cut-off he recklessly claimed to have found suitable for wagons. In fact, Hastings thought better of retracing his eastward approach and ventured down the canyon of Weber River and eventually over the rim. One wagon with its oxen crashed down a precipice. The company following found a better route by taking their wagons down the river, as did the one after that. By 6 August about sixty wagons had got through the high and rugged Wasatch Mountains. That day the Donner party reached the Weber River crossing and found that Hastings had posted a notice.

Eliza Donner:

. . . the Donner Party reached Fort Bridger, and were informed by Hastings's agent that he had gone forward as pilot to a large emigrant train, but had left instructions that all later arrivals should follow his trail. Further, that they would find 'an abundant supply of wood, water, and pasturage along the whole line of road, except one dry drive of thirty miles, or forty at most; that they would have no difficult cañons to pass, and that the road was generally smooth, level, and hard'.

At Fort Bridger, my father took as driver for one of his wagons,

John Baptiste Trubode, a sturdy young mountaineer, the offspring of a French father – a trapper – and a Mexican mother. John claimed to have a knowledge of the languages and customs of various Indian tribes through whose country we should have to pass . . .

The trail from the fort was all that could be desired, and on the third of August, we reached the crossing of Weber River, where it breaks through the mountains into the cañon. There we found a letter from Hastings stuck in the cleft of a projecting stick near the roadside. It advised all parties to encamp and await his return for the purpose of showing them a better way than through the cañon of Weber River, stating that he had found the road over which he was then piloting a train very bad, and feared other parties might not be able to get their wagons through the cañon leading to the valley of the Great Salt Lake.

He referred, however, to another route which he declared to be much better, as it avoided the cañon altogether. To prevent unnecessary delays, Messrs. Reed, Pike, and Stanton volunteered to ride over the new route, and, if advisable, bring Hastings back to conduct us to the open valley. After eight days Mr. Reed returned alone, and reported that he and his companions overtook Hastings with his train near the south end of Salt Lake; that Hastings refused to leave his train, but was finally induced to go with them to the summit of a ridge of the Wahsatch Mountains and from there point out as best he could, the directions to be followed.

While exploring on the way back, Mr. Reed had become separated from Messrs. Pike and Stanton and now feared they might be lost. He himself had located landmarks and blazed trees and felt confident that, by making occasional short clearings, we could get our wagons over the new route as outlined by Hastings. Searchers were sent ahead to look up the missing men, and we immediately broke camp and resumed travel.

The following evening we were stopped by a thicket of quaking ash, through which it required a full day's hard work to open a passageway. Thence our course lay through a wilderness of rugged peaks and rock-bound cañons until a heavily obstructed gulch confronted us. Believing that it would lead out to the Utah River Valley, our men again took their tools and became roadmakers. They had toiled six days, when W. F. Graves, wife, and eight children; J. Fosdick, wife, and child, and John Snyder, with their teams and cattle, overtook and joined our train. With the assistance of these three fresh men, the road, eight miles in length, was completed two days later. It carried us out into a pretty mountain dell, not the opening we had expected.

Fortunately, we here met the searchers returning with Messrs. Pike and Stanton. The latter informed us that we must turn back over our newly made road, and cross a farther range of peaks in order to strike the outlet to the valley. Sudden fear of being lost in the trackless mountains almost precipitated a panic, and it was with difficulty that my father and other cool-headed persons kept excited families from scattering rashly into greater dangers.

We retraced our way, and after five days of alternate traveling and roadmaking, ascended a mountain so steep that six and eight yoke of oxen were required to draw each vehicle up the grade, and most careful handling of the teams was necessary to keep the wagons from toppling over as the straining cattle zigzaged to the summit. Fortunately, the slope on the opposite side was gradual and the last wagon descended to camp before darkness obscured the way.

The following morning, we crossed the river which flows from Utah Lake to Great Salt Lake and found the trail of the Hastings party. We had been thirty days in reaching that point, which we had hoped to make in ten or twelve.[22]

Such delays were responsible for the plight in which the Donner party found themselves on attempting to cross the Sierras two months later.

Eliza Donner:

A new inventory, taken about this time, disclosed the fact that the company's stock of supplies was insufficient to carry it through to California. A call was made for volunteers who should hasten on horseback to Sutter's Fort, secure supplies and, returning, meet the train *en route.* Mr. Stanton, who was without family, and Mr. McCutchen, whose wife and child were in the company, heroically responded. They were furnished with necessaries for their personal needs, and with letters to Captain Sutter, explaining the company's situation, and petitioning for supplies which would enable it to reach the settlement. . . .

In addressing this letter to Captain Sutter, my father followed the general example of emigrants to California in those days, for Sutter, great-hearted and generous, was the man to whom all turned in distress or emergencies. He himself had emigrated to the United States at an early age, and after a few years spent in St. Louis, Missouri, had pushed his way westward to California.

There he negotiated with the Russian Government for its holdings on the Pacific coast, and took them over when Russia evacuated the country. He then established himself on the vast estates so acquired, which, in memory of his parentage, he called New Helvetia. The Mexican Government, however, soon assumed his liabilities to the Russian Government, and exercised sovereignty over the territory. Sutter's position, nevertheless, was practically that of a potentate. He constructed the well-known fort near the present site of the city of Sacramento, as protection against Indian depredations, and it became a trading centre and rendezvous for incoming emigrants.[22]

A few days later the company came upon another trackside communication from Hastings, so torn that at first it was unreadable.

Eliza:

In surprise and consternation, the emigrants gazed at its blank face, then toward the dreary waste beyond. Presently, my mother knelt before it and began searching for fragments of paper, which she believed crows had wantonly pecked off and dropped to the ground.

Spurred by her zeal, others also were soon on their knees, scratching among the grasses and sifting the loose soil through their fingers. What they found, they brought to her, and after the search ended she took the guide board, laid it across her lap, and thoughtfully began fitting the ragged edges of paper together and matching the scraps to marks on the board. The tedious process was watched with spellbound interest by the anxious group around her.

The writing was that of Hastings, and her patchwork brought out the following words: 'Two days – two nights – hard driving – cross – desert – reach water.'

This would be a heavy strain on our cattle, and to fit them for the ordeal they were granted thirty-six hours' indulgence near the bubbling waters [*of a spring*], amid good pasturage. Meanwhile grass was cut and stored, water casks were filled, and rations were prepared for desert use.

We left camp on the morning of September 9, following dimly marked wagon-tracks courageously, and entered upon the 'dry drive', which Hastings and his agent at Fort Bridger had represented as being thirty-five miles, or forty at most. After two days and two nights of continuous travel, over a waste of alkali and sand, we were still surrounded as far as eye could see by a region of fearful desolation. The supply of feed for our cattle was gone, the water casks were empty, and a pitiless sun was turning its burning rays upon the glaring earth over which we still had to go.

Mr. Reed now rode ahead to prospect for water, while the rest followed with the teams. All who could walk did so, mothers carrying their babes in their arms, and fathers with weaklings across their shoulders moved slowly as they urged the famishing cattle forward. Suddenly an outcry of joy gave hope to those whose courage waned. A lake of shimmering water appeared before us in the near distance, we could see the wavy grasses and a caravan of people moving towards it.

'It may be Hastings!' was the eager shout. Alas, as we advanced, the scene vanished! A cruel mirage, in its mysterious way, had outlined the lake and cast our shadows near its shore.

Disappointment intensified our burning thirst, and my good mother gave her own and other suffering children wee lumps of sugar, moistened with a drop of peppermint, and later put a flattened bullet in each child's mouth to engage its attention and help keep the salivary glands in action.

Then followed soul-trying hours. Oxen, footsore and weary, stumbled under their yokes. Women, heartsick and exhausted, could walk no farther. As a last resort, the men hung the water pails on their arms, unhooked the oxen from the wagons, and by persuasion and force, drove them onward, leaving the women and children to await their return. Messrs. Eddy and Graves got their animals to water on the night of the twelfth, and the others later. As soon as the poor beasts were refreshed, they were brought back with water for the suffering, and also that they might draw the wagons on to camp. My father's wagons were the last taken out. They reached camp the morning of the fifteenth.

Thirty-six head of cattle were left on that desert, some dead, some lost. Among the lost were all Mr. Reed's herd, except an ox and a cow. His poor beasts had become frenzied in the night, as they were being driven toward water, and with the strength that comes with madness, had rushed away in the darkness. . . .

After hurriedly making camp, all the men turned out to hunt the Reed cattle. In every direction they searched, but found no clue. Those who rode onward, however, discovered that we had reached only an oasis in the desert, and that six miles ahead of us lay another pitiless barren stretch.

Anguish and dismay now filled all hearts. Husbands bowed their heads, appalled at the situation of their families. Some cursed Hastings for the false statements in his open letter and for his broken pledge at Fort Bridger. They cursed him also for his misrepresentation of the distance across this cruel desert, traversing which had wrought such suffering and loss. . . .

It was plain that, try as we might, we could not get back to Fort Bridger. We must proceed regardless of the fearful outlook.[22]

On 26 September they linked up with the California Trail from Fort Hall. The last company of the people who had taken the established northern route via Fort Hall were already through the Sierra Nevada pass. So much for Hastings's time-saver!

With the Donner party was Irish-born Patrick Breen, his wife, and seven children. Fourteen-years-old John, eldest of the Breen children, recalled how the recurring delays were at last causing grave anxiety . . .

. . . the more so that on the morning of their leaving the long encampment on the desert there appeared a considerable fall of snow on the neighbouring hills. The apprehension of delay from this cause, and of scarcity, made the mothers tremble. But they knew that to give way was to make unavoidable that which they dreaded, and they put the best possible face on to meet their discouragements. The men were irritable and impatient. . . .[6]

On 5 October two teams of oxen tangled in ascending a difficult sandhill on the Humboldt River, and an altercation led to John Snyder, a thirty-five-years-old teamster for 'Uncle Billy' Graves striking James Reed across the forehead with the butt of a whip. Reed retaliated by stabbing Snyder in the chest with a hunting knife, and the latter died in a few minutes. Lewis Keseberg, a huge German, was for hanging the remorseful Reed there and then. Two men stood by Reed: his teamster, Milt Elliott, and William Eddy, travelling with wife and two children, who had abandoned his wagon and now shared with the Reeds. A tense situation was resolved when it was decided that Reed should be banished from the party, leaving behind his wife and children. The Donners at this time were a few miles ahead on the trail. On 8 October Reed caught up with them, explained about the killing, and went ahead on horseback, a teamster called Herron accompanying him on foot.

During the next few days, spent in crossing parched desert country, the party suffered further demoralization. There were two more fatalities. An elderly Belgian named Hardkoop, a single man who had been travelling with the Kesebergs, was put out of the wagon to walk. His feet swelled until the skin split. He twice fell miles behind, the second time never to be seen again. None of the weary travellers was prepared to go back for the old man, though that night Eddy and Milt Elliott kept a camp-fire burning until dawn. Misfortunes piled up for the party. Indians stole horses and cattle, and shot arrows into oxen, which had to be left behind for the culprits to feast on. Loss of oxen led to the abandonment of wagons. Eddy had to abandon Reed's family wagon. Mrs Reed and her children were taken in by the Donners. Another who had to abandon his wagon was a German called Wolfinger. Two bachelors, Reinhart and Spitzer, stayed behind to help the wealthy Wolfinger bury his goods, rejoining the party with news that Wolfinger had been killed by Indians. Few, if any, believed them. The party was reduced to fifteen wagons. The Eddy family had to walk. The kindly Donners took in Mrs Wolfinger.

The nightmare crossing of The Fortymile Desert finally ended, when the party reached the Truckee River. John Breen recalled:

On Truckee River the weather was already very cold, and the heavy clouds hanging over the mountains to the west were strong indications of an approaching winter. This, of course, alarmed several people, while others paid no attention to it. My father's family among the former, used every effort to cross the mountains before the snow became too deep. We traveled up the river a few days, when we met the excellent Stanton, returning with [*two Indian guides and*] five or six mules, packed with flour and meat. John A. Sutter had given him the mules and provisions, for the mere promise of compensation. . . .[6]

Eliza Donner:

In camp that night, Mr. Stanton outlined our course to the settlement, and in compliance with my father's earnest wish, consented to lead the train across the Sierra Nevada Mountains. Frost in the air and snow on the distant peaks warned us against delays; yet, notwithstanding the need of haste, we were obliged to rest our jaded teams. Three yoke of oxen had died from exhaustion within a week, and several of those remaining were not in condition to ascend the heavy grades before them.[22]

Stanton unwisely agreed to their resting five days at Truckee Meadows, during which time a man called Pike was killed in a pistol accident at the camp. Shortly after their resuming the journey, an Indian was shot dead.

Eliza:

My father and uncle took our wagons to the rear of the train in order to favor our cattle, and also to be near families whose teams might need help in getting up the mountains. That day we crossed the Truckee River for the forty-ninth and last time in eighty miles, and encamped for the night at the top of a high hill, where we received our last experience of Indian cruelty. The perpetrator was concealed behind a willow, and with savage vim and well trained hand, sent nineteen arrows whizzing through the air, and each arrow struck a different ox. Mr. Eddy caught him in the act; and as he turned to flee, the white man's rifle ball struck him between the shoulders and pierced his body. With a spring into the air and an agonizing shriek, he dropped lifeless into the bushes below.[22]

When early next morning the train took the trail, they expected to cross the snow-capped Sierras and reach California in less than two

*weeks. A broken axle led to the Donner families being separated from
the rest of the party.*

*Hitherto, arrival at Sutter's Fort had dated the conclusion of the
overland journey to California. Now Johnson's ranch, about forty miles
north of the fort, represented civilization; though Johnson was described
by one emigrant as 'a rough sailor, dwelling in a dirty, little hut, and
surrounded by naked Indians', the latter causing embarrassment to
the white ladies. Bryant's group of young men had got through by 30
August, and the first wagon reached Johnson's on 15 September.
Significantly, they had stuck throughout to the established route. The
last of the people who took the old trail went through the pass about
26 September, and the first of the companies led by Hastings about five
days later. Now only the Donner party remained to get through. The
Breens led the way towards the summit.*

John Breen:

In the morning it was very cold, with about an inch of snow on
the ground. This made us hurry our cattle still more, if possible, than
before. We traveled on, and, at last, the clouds cleared, leaving the
towering peaks in full view, covered as far as the eye could reach with
snow. This sight made us almost despair of ever entering the long-
sought valley of the Sacramento; but we pushed on as fast as our
failing cattle could haul our almost empty wagons. At last we reached
the foot of the main ridge, near Truckee Lake. It was sundown. The
weather was clear in the early part of the night; but a large circle
around the moon indicated, as we rightly supposed, an approaching
storm. Daylight came only to confirm our worst fears. The snow was
falling fast on that terrible summit over which we had yet to make
our way. Notwithstanding, we set out early to make an effort to cross.
We traveled one or two miles – the snow increasing in depth all the
way. At last, it was up to the axles of the wagons. We now concluded
to leave them, pack some blankets on the oxen, and push forward;
but by the time we got the oxen packed, it was impossible to advance;
first, because of the depth of the snow, and next, because we could
not find the road; so we hitched to the wagons and returned to the
valley again, where we found it raining in torrents. We took possession of a cabin and built a fire in it, but the pine boughs were a poor

shelter from the rain, so we turned our cattle at large, and lay down under our wagon-covers to pass the night.

It cleared off in the night, and thus gave us hope; we were so little acquainted with the country as to believe that rain in the valley meant rain in the mountains also, and that it would beat down the snow so that we might possibly go over. In that we were fatally mistaken. We set out next morning to make a last struggle. . . .[6]

They got to within three miles of the summit, before having to turn back. One of the party, Lewis Keseberg, who had injured a foot on the journey, afterwards complained:

When we reached the lake, we lost our road, and owing to the depth of the snow on the mountains, were compelled to abandon our wagons, and pack our goods on oxen. The cattle, unused to such burdens, caused great delay by 'bucking' and wallowing in the snow. There was also much confusion as to what articles should be taken and what abandoned. One wanted a box of tobacco carried along; another, a bale of calico, and some one thing and some another. But for this delay we would have passed the summit and pressed forward to California.

Owing to my lameness, I was placed on horseback, and my foot was tied up to the saddle in a sort of sling. Near evening we were close to the top of the dividing ridge. It was cold and chilly, and everybody was tired with the severe exertions of the day. Some of the emigrants sat down to rest, and declared they could go no further. I begged them for God's sake to get over the ridge before halting. Some one, however, set fire to a pitchy pine tree, and the flames soon ascended to its topmost branches. The women and children gathered about this fire to warm themselves. Meantime the oxen were rubbing off their packs against the trees. The weather looked very threatening, and I exhorted them to go on until the summit was reached. . . . As it was, all lay down on the snow, and from exhaustion were soon asleep. In the night, I felt something impeding my breath. A heavy weight seemed to be resting upon me. Springing up to a sitting posture, I found myself covered with freshly-fallen snow. The camp, the cattle, my companions, had all disappeared. All I could see was snow everywhere. I shouted at the top of my voice. Suddenly, here and there, all about me, heads popped up through the snow. The scene was not unlike what one might imagine at the resurrection, when people rise up out of the earth. The terror amounted to a panic. The mules were lost, the cattle strayed away, and our further progress rendered impossible. . . . We returned to the lake, and prepared, as best we could, for the winter. I was unable to build a cabin, because of my lameness, and so erected a sort of brush shed against one side of Breen's cabin.[26]

The cabin Patrick Breen and family had settled into was that which had sheltered Moses Schallenberger, of the Stevens party, during the winter of '44/45. But the Stevens party had taken wagons over the mountains in late November. And Hastings and some companions had gone through in late December '45, though earning a reprimand from Sutter. The Donner party could consider themselves unlucky that snow should have blocked the pass at the close of October. But one day of the many they squandered on the journey would probably have saved them the ordeal of the following months.

Two camps were set up. At Truckee (later Donner) Lake cabins were built close to the Schallenberger/Breen cabin. The other camp was five miles east, at Alder Creek, where little Eliza Donner watched the men erect shelters for thirteen adults and eight children:

They cleared a space under a tall pine tree and re-set the tent a few feet south of its trunk, facing the sunrise. Then, following the Indian method as described by John Baptiste, a rude semi-circular hut of poles was added to the tent, the tree-trunk forming part of its north wall, and its needled boughs, the rafters and cross-pieces to the roof. The structure was overlaid so far as possible with pieces of cloth, old quilts, and buffalo robes, then with boughs and branches of pine and tamarack. A hollow was scooped in the ground near the tree for a fireplace, and an opening in the top served as chimney and ventilator. One opening led into the tent and another served as an outer door.

To keep the beds off the wet earth, two rows of short posts were driven along the sides in the tent, and poles were led across the tops, thus forming racks to support the pine boughs upon which the beds should be made. . . .

The combination of tent and hut was designed for my father and family and Mrs. Wolfinger. The teamsters, Samuel Shoemaker, Joseph Reinhart, James Smith, and John Baptiste, built their hut in Indian wigwam fashion. Not far from us, across the stream, braced against a log, was reared a mixed structure of brush and tent for use of Uncle Jacob, Aunt Betsy, and William and Solomon Hook (Aunt Betsy's sons by a former husband), and their five small children, George, Mary, Isaac, Lewis, and Samuel Donner. . . .

When we awoke the following morning, little heaps of snow lay here and there upon the floor. No threshold could be seen, only a snow-bank reaching up to the white plain beyond, where every sound was muffled, and every object was blurred by falling flakes.[22]

On 12 November an abortive attempt was made by thirteen of the men and two women to cross the pass. Nine days later a larger party, sixteen males and six females, tried and failed. Heavy snow fell steadily for eight days, until only the roofs of the cabins showed. All the remaining oxen, horses and mules strayed and perished. The temperature fell to far below zero.

Patrick, head of the Irish Breens, began keeping a diary on 20 November. On 6 December he wrote:

The morning fine & Clear   now some cloudy   wind S–E
    not [melting] much in the sunshine,   Stanton & Graves manufactureing snow shoes for another mountain scrabble   no account of mules[7]

And again on Sunday 13th:

Snows faster than any previous day   wind N:W   Stanton & Graves with several others makeing preperations to cross the Mountains on snow shoes,   snow 8 feet deep on the level   dull[7]

Then on the 16th:

fair & pleasant   froeze hard last night & the company started on snow shoes to cross the mountains   wind S.E   looks pleasant[7]

The day before, one of Reed's hired men died, the first death at Truckee Lake camp.

The Snow-shoe Party was composed of ten men, two boys, and five women. Women were already demonstrating their superior powers of survival. Each person carried one blanket or quilt; there was no change of clothing. They had one hatchet, and a few guns. The meagre rations Stanton hoped would last six days. The eldest of the Graves's eight children, Mary, aged twenty, penned a reminiscence of the snow-shoe trek:

We had a very slavish day's travel, climbing the divide. Nothing of interest occurred until reaching the summit. The scenery was too grand for me to pass without notice, the changes being so great; walking now on loose snow, and now stepping on a hard, slick rock a number of hundred yards in length. Being a little in the rear of the party, I had a chance to observe the company ahead, trudging along with packs on their backs. It reminded me of some Norwegian fur company among the icebergs. My shoes were ox-bows, split in two, and rawhide strings woven in, something in form of the old-fashioned, split-bottomed chairs. Our clothes were of the bloomer costume, and generally were made of flannel. Well do I remember a remark one of the company made here, that we were about as near heaven as we could get. We camped a little on the west side of the summit the second night.[20]

On the first day they had travelled about four miles; on the second day six miles. On the third day progress was still exhausting, even though slightly downhill. Several of the party were suffering from snow blindness. When they camped that night, the small and lightly-boned Stanton was missing; he struggled into camp an hour later. On the fourth day snow squalls made conditions even worse than before. Mary Graves suffered an hallucination:

Observing by the way a deep gorge at the right, having the appearance of being full of smoke, I wanted very much to go to it, but the Indians said no, that was not the way. I prevailed on the men to fire the gun, but there was no answer. Every time we neared the gorge I would halloo at the top of my voice, but we received no answer.[20]

On the fifth day Stanton again came into camp an hour behind the others. When the party left camp next morning, Stanton was sitting by the fire smoking his pipe. He told Mary Graves: 'I am coming soon.' But they did not see him again. Charles Stanton, aged thirty-five, from Chicago, had made errors of judgment; but, though a single man with no family left behind, he had kept his promise to come back from

California and help his companions; and he died with a dignity later associated with Captain Oates in the Antarctic.

On the sixth day the food ran out, and the two Indian guides lost the way. The party struggled on, half-frozen and starving. There was only one answer to their mad hunger: human flesh. They considered drawing lots for who should be the first to be killed and eaten; Eddy suggested a six-shooter duel. In the end it was decided they should continue the journey: they were so weak that natural causes would soon solve their moral dilemma. The first to die was a Mexican herdsman called Antonio, then 'Uncle Billy' Graves, both on Christmas Eve. On Christmas Day, Patrick Dolan, a bachelor, died, and it was his limbs that provided the first human flesh for roasting. Eddy and the Indians turned away, but the others ate, weeping and averting their faces from each other. A thirteen-years-old boy, Lemuel Murphy, died on the 26th. They rested three days. The two Indians ate on the second day. Only Eddy refused to eat. One rule of decorum was observed, as it was at the snow-bound camps at Truckee Lake and Alder Creek – one did not eat the flesh of a member of one's own family.

The snow-shoe trek got under way again. That evening William Eddy experienced the first signs of a coma into which he knew he would sink and die if he did not eat. He ate the only food available, and his strength returned. Of this stage of the journey Mary Graves recollected:

Our only chance for camp-fire for the night was to hunt a dead tree of some description, and set fire to it. The hemlock being the best and generally much the largest timber, it was our custom to select the driest we could find without leaving our course. When the fire would reach the top of the tree, the falling limbs would fall all around us and bury themselves in the snow, but we heeded them not. Sometimes the falling, blazing limbs would brush our clothes, but they never hit us; that would have been too lucky a hit. We would sit or lie on the snow, and rest our weary frames. We would sleep, only to dream of something nice to eat, and awake again to disappointment. Such was our sad fate! Even the reindeer's wretched lot was not worse! 'His dinner and his bed were snow, and supper he had not.' Our fare was the same! We would strike fire by means of the flint-lock gun which we had with us. This had to be carried by

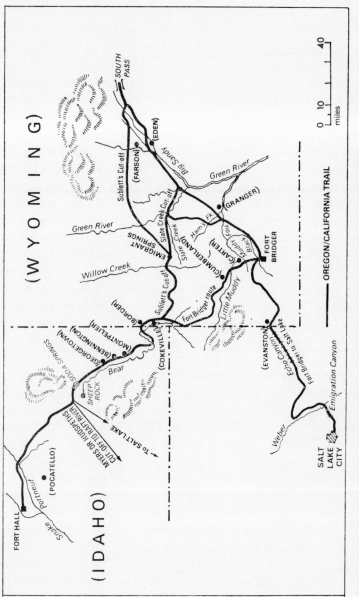

6. The Oregon/California Trail. From the South Pass to Fort Hall, showing the cut-offs and the Mormon route to Salt Lake City

turns, as it was considered the only hope left in case we might find game which we could kill. We traveled over a ridge of mountains, and then descended a deep canyon, where one could scarcely see the bottom. Down, down we would go, or rather slide, for it is very slavish work going down hill, and in many cases we were compelled to slide on our shoes as sleds. On reaching the bottom we would plunge into the snow, so that it was difficult getting out, with the shoes tied to our feet, our packs lashed to our backs, and ourselves head and ears under the snow. But we managed to get out some way, and one by one reached the bottom of the canyon. When this was accomplished we had to ascend a hill as steep as the one we descended. We would drive the toes of our shoes into the loose snow, to make a sort of step, and one by one, as if ascending stair-steps, we climbed up. It took us an entire day to reach the top of the mountain. Each time we attained the summit of a mountain, we hoped we should be able to see something like a valley, but each time came disappointment, for far ahead was always another and higher mountain. We found some springs, or, as we called them, wells, from five to twenty feet under ground, as you might say, for they were under the snow on which we walked. The water was so warm that it melted the snow, and from some of these springs were large streams of running water. We crossed numbers of these streams on bridges of snow, which would sometimes form upon a blade of grass hanging over the water; and from so small a foundation would grow a bridge from ten to twenty-five feet high, and from a foot and a half to three feet across the top. It would make you dizzy to look down at the water, and it was with much difficulty we could place our clumsy ox-bow snow-shoes one ahead of the other without falling. Our feet had been frozen and thawed so many times that they were bleeding and sore. When we stopped at night we would take off our shoes, which by this time were so badly rotted by constant wetting and snow, that there was very little left of them. In the morning we would push our shoes on, bruising and numbing the feet so badly that they would ache and ache with walking and the cold, until night would come again. Oh! the pain! It seemed to make the pangs of hunger more excruciating.[20]

Hunger was again a pressing problem. Now some of the white men were saying that the two Indians should be shot for food. Eddy warned the guides, and they escaped from camp. Eddy took the party's only rifle and went off to look for game. Mary Graves went with him. Luck came their way: Eddy shot a large buck, cut its throat, and he and the girl knelt down and drank the warm blood flowing from the wound.

The venison came too late to save the life of another of the men, Jay Fosdick. When the party overtook the two Indian guides, lying helpless on the snow, William Foster, married to one of the Murphy girls, shot both men and cut them up for food. Even so, the group was soon unable to stumble along on their frost-bitten feet.

Again it was William Eddy who summoned up reserves of strength to go on alone and arrive at a dwelling erected near Johnson's ranch by a family waiting until spring to move deeper into California. A relief party was soon organized to get out to the exhausted people Eddy had left behind that morning.

During the four weeks of the Snow-shoe Party's trek there had been deaths at both the snowbound camps in the Sierras. Eliza Donner describes those at the eastern camp :

Uncle Jacob, the first to die, was older than my father, and had been in miserable health for years before we left Illinois. . . .

My father and mother watched with him during the last night, and the following afternoon helped to lay his body in a cave dug in the mountain side, beneath the snow. That snow had scarcely resettled when Samuel Shoemaker's life ebbed away in happy delirium. He imagined himself a boy again in his father's house and thought his mother had built a fire and set before him the food of which he was fondest. But when Joseph Reinhart's end drew near, his mind wandered, and his whitening lips confessed a part in Mr. Wolfinger's death; and my father, listening, knew not how to comfort that troubled soul. He could not judge whether the self-condemning words were the promptings of a guilty conscience, or the ravings of an unbalanced mind.

Like a tired child falling asleep, was James Smith's death; . . .

During the bitterest weather, we little ones were kept in bed, and my place was always in the middle where Frances and Georgia, snuggling up close, gave me of their warmth, . . .[22]

By the middle of January the snow was twelve to fourteen feet deep around the simple shelters. Eliza resumes:

Nothing could be seen of our abode except the coils of smoke that found their way up through the opening . . . each day John Baptiste climbed to the topmost bough of a tall pine tree and, with straining eyes, scanned the desolate expanse for one moving speck in the distance, for one ruffled track on the snow which should ease our awful suspense.

Days passed. No food in camp except an unsavory beef hide – pinching hunger called for more. Again John Baptiste and Noah James went forth in anxious search for marks of our buried cattle. They made excavations, then forced their hand-poles deep, deeper into the snow, but in vain their efforts – the nail and hook at the points brought up no sign of blood, hair, or hide. In dread unspeakable they returned, and said: 'We shall go mad; we shall die! It is useless to hunt for the cattle; but the *dead*, if they could be reached, their bodies might keep us alive!'

'No,' replied father and mother, speaking for themselves. 'No, part of a hide still remains. When it is gone we will perish, if that be the alternative.'

The fact was, our dead could not have been disturbed even had the attempt been made, for the many snowfalls of winter were banked about them firm as granite walls, and in that camp was neither implement nor arm strong enough to reach their resting-places.[22]

During the first week in January, Mrs Reed, her eldest daughter, a hired girl, and teamster Milt Elliott had made an attempt to get through the pass, but they had been forced back to the lakeside camp, after nearly perishing during four nights in the snow. Unknown to his wife and the others, two months earlier James Reed had tried to get through the pass from the west with provisions. With him was William McCutchen, another original member of the Donner party, who had gone ahead with Stanton in September. Though at times they trudged through snow up to their necks, the two men finally had to admit honourable defeat. On 2 January James Reed took part in the skirmish at Santa Clara between

Americans and the Mexican Californians, and after American supremacy was secured Reed went to Yerba Buena (later San Francisco) and was active in organizing relief for the Donner party. He was responsible for a memorial which read:

To his Excellency, R. F. Stockton, Governor and Commander-in-Chief, by sea and land, of the United States Territory of California: We, the undersigned citizens and residents of the Territory of California, beg leave respectfully to present to your Excellency the following memorial, viz.: That, whereas, the last detachment of emigrants from the United States to California have been unable, from unavoidable causes, to reach the frontier settlements, and are now in the California mountains, seventy-five or one hundred miles east from the Sacramento Valley, surrounded by snow, most probably twenty feet deep, and being about eighty souls in number, a large proportion of whom are women and children, who must shortly be in a famishing condition from scarcity of provisions, therefore, the undersigned most earnestly beseech your Excellency to take into consideration the propriety of fitting out an expedition to proceed on snow-shoes immediately to the relief of the sufferers. Your memorialists beg leave to subscribe themselves, very respectfully, yours, etc.

January, 1847.[32]

From the California Star, *a newspaper published in Yerba Buena, 13 February 1847:*

A company of twenty men left here on Sunday last for the California mountains, with provisions, clothing, etc., for the suffering emigrants now there. The citizens of this place subscribed about 1,500 dollars for their relief, which was expended on such articles as the emigrants would be most likely to need. Mr. Greenwood, an old mountaineer, went with the company as pilot. If it is possible to cross the mountains, they will get to the emigrants in time to save them.[11]

As the Reed/Greenwood relief party left Yerba Buena another party, from Sutter's Fort, was already tackling the pass. The grim situation of the people at the lake camp during these early days of February was tersely recorded by Patrick Breen in his diary:

Frid. 5th   snowd hard all [yesterday] untill 12 o'clock at night
wind still continud to blow hard from the S.W: to day
pretty clear a few clouds only   Peggy [*Mrs Breen*] very uneasy
for fear we shall all perrish with hunger   we have but a little meat
& only part of 3 hides   has to support Mrs. Reid [*Reed*] she has
nothing left but one hide & it is on Graves shanty   Milt [*Elliott*]
is livi[n]g there & likely will keep that hide   Eddys child died
last night.

Satd. 6th   it snowd. faster last night & to day than it has done
this winter & still Continues without an intermission   wind S.W.
Murphys folks or Keysburgs [*Keseberg's*] say they cant eat
hides I wish we had enough of them   Mrs. Eddy very weak.

Sund. 7th   Ceasd. to snow last [night] after one of the most
Severe Storms we experienced this winter   the snow fell about
4 feet deep.   I had to shovel the snow off our shanty this morning
it thawd so fast & thawd. during the whole storm. to day it is quite
pleasant   wind S.W.   Milt here to day says Mrs Reid has to
get a hide from Mrs. Murphy & McCutchins [*McCutchen's*] child
died 2nd of this month.

Mond. 8th   fine clear morning   wind S.W.   froze hard
last. [night]   Spitzer died last night about 3 o clock   to [day?] we
will bury him in the snow   Mrs Eddy died on the night of the 7th.

Tuesd. 9th.   Mrs. Murphy here this morning   pikes child
all but dead   Milt at Murphys not able to get out of bed
Keyburg never gets up says he is not able   John [*Breen*] went
down to day to bury Mrs Eddy & child   heard nothing from
Graves for 2 or 3 days   Mrs Murphy just now going to Graves
fine mor[n]ing   wind S.E.   froze hard last night
begins to thaw in the sun.

Wednsd. 10th   beautiful morning   wind W: froze hard last
night, to day thawing in the sun   Milt Elliot[t] died las[t] night
at Murphys Shanty about 9 o clock P:M: Mrs Reid went there
this morning to see after his effects.   J Denton trying to borrow
meat for Graves   had none to give they have nothing but hides
all are entirely out of meat but a little we have   our hides are
nearly all eat up but with Gods help spring will soon smile upon us.[7]

The relief party from Sutter's began as ten men: three gave up, but the remaining seven got through on snow-shoes to the camp at Truckee lake on 18 February. All seven men were strangers to the stranded people, which makes their achievement even more praiseworthy. Aquilla Glover, Sept Moultry, and 'Dan' Tucker were emigrants to California. Brothers John and Daniel Rhoads had entered California as members of a party of Mormons. Ned Coffeemeyer and Joseph Sels had been sailors. Three of the relief group went on to the Donners' tents and brought back to the lake camp four of the older children, plus Mrs Wolfinger and the teamster, Noah James. Left behind at Alder Creek were a sick George Donner, his wife Tamsen, hired man Jean Baptiste Trubode, Mrs Jacob Donner, and eight children.

On 22 February twenty-four people from the camps – three men, four women, and seventeen children, the three youngest each three years old – were led west by the relief party. The youngest children had to be carried. That same day Reed's relief party was setting out from Johnson's ranch in an easterly direction. Fifteen people were left behind at the lake.

Packs of beef had been cached along the route, but bears got some of the food, and conditions were severe, especially for the children. Two of the Reed children were so weak that they had to be sent back to the cabins. Keseberg's three-years-old daughter died. And an Englishman called Denton lay down in a quilt on the snow and composedly waited for death.

Virginia Reed was twelve years old. Shortly after her rescue she wrote to a cousin:

all of us started and went a piece and Martha and Thomas give out and the men had to take them back   Ma and Eliza and James and I come on and o Mary that was the hades [*hardest*] thing yet to come on and leiv them thar   did not now but what thay would starve to Death   Martha said well Ma if you never see me again do the best you can   the men said they could hardly stand it   it maid them all cry but they said it was better for all of us to go on for if we was to go back we would eat that much more from them   thay give them a little meat and flore and took them back and we come on   we went over great hye mountain as strait as stair steps in snow up to our knees   litle James walk the hole way over all the mountain in snow up to his waist. he said every step he took was a gitting nigher Pa and something to eat   the Bears took the provision the men had cashed and we had but very little to eat   when we had traveld 5 days travel we me[t] Pa with 13 men going to the cabins o Mary you do not now how glad we was to see him   we had not seen him for 6 months   we thought we woul never see him again . . .³⁸

Eliza Donner:

After the departure of the First Relief we who were left in the mountains began to watch and pray for the coming of the Second Relief, as we had before watched and prayed for the coming of the First. . . .

With me sitting on her lap, and Frances and Georgia at either side, [my mother] referred to father's illness and lonely condition, and said that when the next 'Relief' came, we little ones might be taken to the settlement, without either parent, but, God willing, both would follow later. . . .

Often her eyes gazed wistfully to westward, where sky and mountains seemed to meet, and she told us that beyond those snowy peaks lay California, our land of food and safety, our promised land of happiness, where God would care for us. Oh, it was painfully quiet some days in those great mountains, and lonesome upon the snow. The pines had a whispering homesick murmur, and we children had lost all inclination to play.

The last food which I remember seeing in our camp before the arrival of the Second Relief was a thin mould of tallow, which mother had pried out of the trimmings of the jerked beef brought us by the First Relief. She had let it harden in a pan, and after all other rations had given out, she cut daily from it three small white squares for each of us, and we nibbled off the four corners very slowly, and then around and around the edges of the precious pieces until they became too small for us to hold between our fingers.²²

Then, when the Reed party arrived:

When my father learned that the Second Relief comprised only ten men, he felt that he himself would never reach the settlement. He was willing to be left alone, and entreated mother to leave him and try to save herself and us children. He reminded her that his life was almost spent, that she could do little for him were she to remain, and that in caring for us children she would be carrying on his work.

She who had to choose between the sacred duties of wife and mother, thought not of self. She looked first at her helpless little children, then into the face of her suffering and helpless husband, and tenderly, unhesitatingly, announced her determination to remain and to care for him until both should be rescued, or death should part them. . . .

Mother, fearing that we children might not survive another storm in camp, begged Messrs. Cady and Stone to take us with them, offering them five hundred dollars in coin, to deliver us to Elitha and Leanna at Sutter's Fort. The agreement was made, and she collected a few keepsakes and other light articles, which she wished us to have, and which the men seemed more than willing to carry out of the mountains. Then, lovingly, she combed our hair and helped us to dress quickly for the journey. When we were ready, except cloak and hood, she led us to the bedside, and we took leave of father. The men helped us up the steps and stood us up on the snow. She came, put on our cloaks and hoods, saying, as if talking to herself, 'I may never see you again, but God will take care of you.'[22]

The second relief party returned through the pass with three Donner children, the remaining two Reed children, and the Breen and Graves families. One of Jacob Donner's youngsters died on the trek. The party met William Eddy and William Foster, bringing provisions from Sutter's. On reaching Truckee Lake each man learned that a son had died and the corpse's flesh cooked and eaten. Eddy offered to take out those strong enough to travel. Tamsen Donner refused to leave her dying husband, and herself died. Keseberg and old Mrs Murphy were not fit to travel.

When in April a third relief party reached Truckee Lake, only Lewis Keseberg still lived to be rescued. Years later he told C. F. McGlashan, who was investigating the Donner Party tragedy:

A heavy storm came on . . . Mrs. George Donner had remained with her sick husband in their camp, six or seven miles away. Mrs.

Murphy lived about a week after we were left alone. When my provisions gave out, I remained four days before I could taste human flesh. There was no other resort – it was that or death. . . . The flesh of starved beings contains little nutriment. It is like feeding straw to horses. I cannot describe the unutterable repugnance with which I tasted the first mouthful of flesh. . . . A man, before he judges me, should be placed in a similar situation; . . .[26]

Concerning Tamsen Donner, Keseberg told McGlashan:

At midnight, one cold, bitter night, Mrs. George Donner came to my door. It was about two weeks after Reed had gone, and my loneliness was beginning to be unendurable. I was most happy to hear the sound of a human voice. Her coming was like that of an angel from heaven. But she had not come to bear me company. Her husband had died in her arms. She had remained by his side until death came, and then had laid him out and hurried away. He died at nightfall, and she had traveled over the snow alone to my cabin. She was going, alone, across the mountains. She was going to start without food or guide. She kept saying: 'My children! I must see my children!' She feared she would not survive, and told me she had some money in her tent. It was too heavy for her to carry. She said, 'Mr. Keseberg, I confide this to your care.' She made me promise sacredly that I would get the money and take it to her children in case she perished and I survived. She declared she would start over the mountains in the morning. She said, 'I am bound to go to my children.' She seemed very cold, and her clothes were like ice. I think she had got in the creek in coming. She said she was very hungry, but refused the only food I could offer. She had never eaten the loathsome flesh. She finally lay down, and I spread a feather-bed and some blankets over her. In the morning she was dead. I think the hunger, the mental suffering, and the icy chill of the preceding night, caused her death. I have often been accused of taking her life. Before my God, I swear this is untrue! . . . There were plenty of corpses lying around. . . .[26]

Thirty-four emigrants had died at the camps or in the mountains. Irving Stone, in his book Men to Match my Mountains: The Opening of the Far West 1840-1900 (*London 1967, p. 94*), *most eloquently sums up the disaster: 'The Donner Party has a mystical meaning in the settlement of the Far West: it is Greek tragedy, moving one to pity and terror, the bloodletting* par excellence*; the ultimate cup of grief into which all of the tears avoided by former parties are shed. All of the bad judgment and bad luck somehow skirted by the others is heaped upon the hapless heads of the one party on whom the furies pour their pent-up vengeance at having been cheated of their victims these five long years during which dumb, stumbling men had overcome the unscalable mountains, unendurable salt and sand deserts. It is the ultimate tragedy without which no distant frontier can be conquered; and which gives a structural base of blood and bone and suffering and sacrifice and, in a sense, of redemption, to a new people creating a new life in a new world.'*

But there was, too, a practical benefit arising out of the Donner Party's experience. In cutting their way through the Wasatch Mountains they opened a route to be taken by other emigrants to California, and by the Mormons who in the following year sought escape from persecution and a place for settlement.

Westward with God:
The Mormons,
1846/7

The great movement west of members of the Church of Jesus Christ of Latter-day Saints – one of the most remarkable treks in history – which ended in their finding Zion in Salt Lake Valley in 1847, can be said to have begun in February 1846 with the evacuation of the prosperous city they had created at Nauvoo, Illinois. This was the third time in their brief history that the Saints had been forced from a settlement by hostile non-Mormons.

The Church of Jesus Christ of Latter-day Saints had been established in April 1830, at Fayette, New York, by Joseph Smith, son of a Vermont farmer. In July of the preceding year Smith had completed The Book of Mormon – translations, he said, of inscriptions on gold plates found on the Hill Cumorah, near Palmyra, N.Y., to which he had been directed by an angel named Moroni, son of Mormon, last of the Nephites, a tribe who had reached America from Jerusalem about 600 B.C. The Saints soon became much more than just another religious sect: they became a people, and believed they were specially chosen and favoured by God. They were a tightly-organized community, whose leader could use their block vote to bargain politically. They referred to non-Mormons as 'Gentiles'. They often acted as though they were a law unto themselves. They met with opposition from non-Mormons, at times violent.

Their first community was set up at Kirtland, Ohio, from which they were driven to found another at Independence, in Jackson County, in frontier Missouri. Again there were clashes with 'Gentiles', barn-burnings and killings. In October 1838, Governor Lilburn Boggs ordered out six thousand men of the state militia against the Mormons.

This time the Saints founded a new town on an Illinois bank of the Mississippi. Prophet Joseph Smith named it Nauvoo. It grew rapidly: from three hundred inhabitants on its founding in 1839 to seven thousand by 1842, and about fifteen thousand by 1845. Smith

obtained a charter from the state which virtually gave Nauvoo autono-
mous rule, defended by their own militia.

But again there were clashes with non-Mormons. And the Mormons
were themselves split over the issue of plural wives. Smith was opposed
on this issue by a group who established their own newspaper, the
Nauvoo Expositor. *When Smith tried to destroy the rival press, he*
and his brother Hyrum were arrested and lodged in jail at the town of
Carthage. On 27 June 1844, an anti-Mormon mob broke into the jail
and shot dead the Smith brothers.

The ensuing struggle for leadership of the Saints was won by Brigham
Young, aged forty-three years, a man of strong personality and
considerable organizing ability.

Feeling was running high against the Mormons at Nauvoo. They
received a crushing blow when the Illinois legislature revoked the charter
granted to the Saints. Young saw that if the Mormons were to develop
unmolested their community, institutions, and religion, they should
seek an isolated place in which to settle. The obvious place was somewhere
well beyond the western frontier. Joseph Smith had spoken a few years
before of sending an expedition beyond the Rocky Mountains to seek
out a place in which the Saints could establish a settlement where they
would not be harried by enemies. In September 1845, Brigham Young
and his Council of Twelve met Illinois officials and agreed to start evacu-
ating Nauvoo during the spring of 1846.

A circular of the High Council, published on 20 January 1846, in-
formed Saints throughout the world that their brethren at Nauvoo had
resolved to seek a new home beyond the Rocky Mountains.

Beloved Brethren and Friends, We, the members of the High
Council of the Church, by the voice of all her authorities, have
unitedly and unanimously agreed, and embrace this opportunity
to inform you, that we intend to set out into the Western country
from this place, some time in the early part of the month of March,
a company of pioneers, consisting mostly of young, hardy men,
with some families. These are destined to be furnished with an
ample outfit; taking with them a printing press, farming utensils of
all kinds, with mill irons and bolting cloths, seeds of all kinds, grain,
&c.

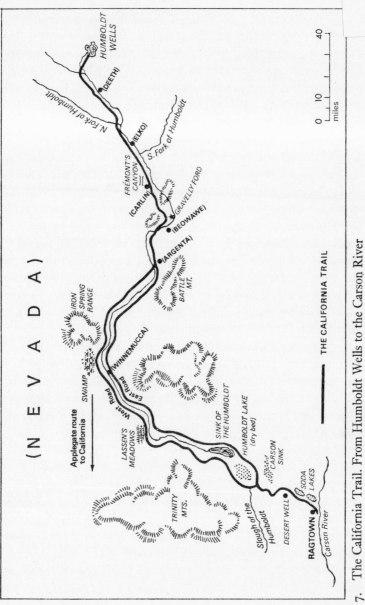

7. The California Trail. From Humboldt Wells to the Carson River

The object of this early move is, to put in a spring crop, to build houses, and to prepare for the reception of families who will start so soon as grass shall be sufficiently grown to sustain teams and stock. Our pioneers are instructed to proceed West till they find a good place to make a crop, in some good valley in the neighborhood of the Rocky Mountains, where they will infringe upon no one, and be not likely to be infringed upon. Here we will make a resting place, until we can determine a place for a permanent location. . . .

Much of our property will be left in the hands of competent agents for sale at a low rate, for teams, for goods, and for cash. The funds arising from the sale of property will be applied to the removal of families from time to time as fast as consistent, and it now remains to be proven whether those of our families and friends who are necessarily left behind for a season to obtain an outfit, through the sale of property, shall be mobbed, burnt, and driven away by force. Does any American want the honor of doing it? or will Americans suffer such acts to be done, and the disgrace of them to rest on their character under existing circumstances? If they will, let the world know it. But we do not believe they will.

We agreed to leave the country for the sake of peace, upon the condition that no more vexatious prosecutions be instituted against us. In good faith we have labored to fulfil this engagement. Governor Ford has also done his duty to further our wishes in this respect. But there are some who are unwilling that we should have an existence anywhere. But our destinies are in the hands of God, and so also is theirs. . . .[27]

As opposition to the Mormons intensified – more than one hundred and fifty homes had been destroyed on the outskirts of Nuvoo – Young decided to start the exodus before winter had ended. There was ice on the Mississippi when the evacuation began on 4 February. Cabins were constructed at Sugar Creek, on the Iowa side of the river, as a temporary station, called Camp of Israel. Addressing the Saints at Sugar Creek on 17 February, Brigham Young announced that advance parties would create rest stations at stages on the way across Iowa to the frontier, whence the Saints would eventually take to the plains. Their final destination was not revealed, but, Young assured his congregation, 'the angels of God will go with you, even as they went with the children of Israel when Moses led them from the land of Egypt'.

The Saints moved west. In April they reached Garden Grove, about halfway across Iowa, where they set up a station. On 11 May Young pressed on with three to four thousand people. Another rest station was set up, at Mount Pisgah. On 14 June Young reached the Missouri River, a little south of Council Bluffs. After making arrangements for another station on the Iowa side of the river, Young ferried over into Nebraska, and established Winter Quarters (now Florence).

Colonel Thomas L. Kane, who belonged to a distinguished Philadelphia family and became sympathetic to the Mormons after attending one of their meetings, visited the frontier Mormon camp at Council Bluffs.

They were collected a little distance above the Pottawatamie agency. The hills of the 'High Prairie' crowding in upon the river at this point, and overhanging it, appear of an unusual and commanding elevation. They are called the Council Bluffs, a name given them with another meaning, but well illustrated by the picturesque congress of their high and mighty summits. To the south of them, a rich alluvial flat of considerable width follows down the Missouri, some eight miles, to where it is lost from view at a turn, which forms the sight of the Indian town of Point Aux Poules. Across the river from this spot the hills recur again, but are skirted at their base by as much low ground as suffices for a landing.

This landing, and the large flat or bottom on the east side of the river, were crowded with covered carts and wagons; and each one of the Council Bluff hills opposite was crowned with its own great camp, gay with bright, white canvas, and alive with the busy stir of swarming occupants. In the clear blue morning air, the smoke streamed up from more than a thousand cooking-fires. Countless roads and by-paths checkered all manner of geometric figures on the hill-sides. Herd-boys were dozing upon the slopes; sheep and horses, cows and oxen, were feeding around them, and other herds in the luxuriant meadow of the then swollen river. From a single point I counted four thousand head of cattle in view at one time. As I approached the camps, it seemed to me the children there were to prove still more numerous. Along a little creek I had to cross were women in greater force than *blanchisseuses* upon the Seine, washing and rinsing all manner of white muslins, red flannels and parti-colored calicoes, and hanging them to bleach upon a greater area of grass and bushes than we can display in all our Washington Square.[24]

One day in the fall of 1846 Father Pierre Jean de Smet rode into Winter Quarters. He recorded that Young and his associates asked him 'a thousand questions about the regions I had explored', and in particular they had shown interest when he described the valley of the Salt Lake.

On 14 January 1847, Young proclaimed that God had called on him to lead his people west that spring to seek out their Zion.

Young appointed a historian for the journey, an English convert. William Clayton, born in Lancashire on 17 July 1814, had been ordained a Mormon priest in 1837, and a high priest in the following year. With his wife, he left England and reached Nauvoo in November 1840. He became secretary to Joseph Smith, and later Treasurer at Nauvoo. His journal provides the most detailed record of the journey by which the Saints found their final home. He wrote of the formation of the pioneer party who would make history:

There are 143 men and boys on the list of the pioneer company, three women and Lorenzo Young's two children. . . . There were 72 wagons, 93 horses, 52 mules, 66 oxen, 19 cows, and 17 dogs, and chickens.

The names of the females in this camp are: Harriet Page Young, Clarissa Decker, and Ellen Sanders. The names of the children are Isaac Perry Decker Young and Sabisky L. Young, making a total of 148 souls who have started to go west of the mountains as pioneers to find a home where the saints can live in peace and enjoy the fruits of their labors, and where we shall not be under the dominion of gentile governments, subject to the wrath of mobs and where the standards of peace can be raised, the Ensign to nations reared and the kingdom of God flourish until truth shall prevail, and the saints enjoy the fulness of the gospel.[13]

Brigham Young presided militarily over the company as Lieutenant-General. His orders for the journey were recorded by William Clayton:

'After we start from here, every man must keep his loaded gun in his hand, or in the wagon where he can put his hand on it at a moment's warning. If they are cap locks, take off the cap and put on a little leather to keep wet and etc. out. If flint locks, take out the priming and fill the pan with twine or cotton,' etc. The wagons must keep together when traveling, and not separate as they have previously done, and every man to walk beside his own wagon, and not leave it only by permission. . . . At 5:00 in the morning the bugle is to be sounded as a signal for every man to arise and attend prayers before he leaves his wagon. Then cooking, eating, feeding teams, etc., till seven o'clock, at which time the camp is to move at the sound of the bugle. Each teamster to keep beside his team, with his loaded gun in his hands or in his wagon where he can get it in a moment. The extra men, each to walk opposite his wagon with his loaded gun on his shoulder, and no man to be permitted to leave his wagon unless he obtains permission from his officer. In case of an attack from Indians or hostile appearances, the wagons to travel in double file. The order of encampment to be in a circle with the mouth of the wagon to the outside, and the horses and stock tied inside the circle. At 8:30 p.m. the bugle to be sounded again at which time all to have prayers in their wagons and to retire to rest by nine o'clock.[13]

When the company came upon a Pawnee village of upwards of a hundred lodges, Clayton records that the Mormons were at once cautious:

At 1:00 p.m. the encampment was formed on the bank of the lake and a guard instantly placed at the passes, as many of the Indians had followed us, although they had to wade the river, but it is very shoal. One of the Indians presented several certificates from persons who had previously traveled through their village, all certifying that the Grand Chief of the Pawnees was friendly disposed, and they had made him presents of a little powder, lead, salt, etc. Heber gave them a little tobacco, and a little salt. President Young gave to the chief, some powder, lead, salt and a number of the brethren gave a little flour each. The old chief, however, did not seem to think the presents sufficient, and said he did not like us to go west through their country, he was afraid we should kill their buffalo and drive them off. Brother Shumway told him we did not like buffalo, but this did not appear to give him much satisfaction. However, there was no appearance of hostility. In fact, all that came to camp seemed highly pleased to shake hands with our brethren and would run from one side to another so as not to miss one. A number of the squaws were on the opposite side of the lake with mattocks digging roots. Brother Shumway says there are about twelve thousand of the Pawnees in this neighborhood, and it is reported that there are five thousand warriors.

Though there was no evidence yet of Indian hostility, the company maintained their alert guard. They had one cannon, which was prepared for action, and stood all night just outside the wagons. On the 26th some Indians approached stealthily and some shots were fired at them. Later in the day two horses were stolen.

When herds of buffaloes were spotted on 1 May, Brigham Young ordered a hunt, despite the denial of interest in buffalo meat that had been given to the Pawnee Indian chief. In a chase lasting three hours, one bull, three cows, and six calves were killed.

Clayton was keeping an estimate of the number of miles travelled, and on 8 May recorded in his journal:

I have counted the revolutions of a wagon wheel to tell the exact distance we have traveled. The reason why I have taken this method which is somewhat tedious, is because there is generally a difference of two and sometimes four miles in a day's travel between my estimation and that of some others, and they have all thought I underrated it. This morning I determined to take pains to know for a certainty how far we travel today. Accordingly I measured the circumferenc of the nigh hind wheel of one of Brother Kimball's wagons being the one I sleep in, in charge of Philo Johnson. I found the wheel 14 feet 8 inches in circumference, not varying one eighth of an inch. I then calculated how many revolutions it would require for one mile and found it precisely 360 not varying one fraction which somewhat astonished me. I have counted the whole revolutions during the day's travel and I find it to be a little over eleven and a quarter miles, – twenty revolutions over. The overplus I shall add to the next day's travel. According to my previous calculations we were two hundred eighty-five miles from Winter Quarters this morning before we started. After traveling ten miles I placed a small cedar post in the ground with these words written on it with a pencil. 'From Winter Quarters, two hundred ninety-five miles, May 8, '47. Camp all well. Wm. Clayton.' . . . I have repeatedly suggested a plan of fixing machinery to a wagon wheel to tell the exact distance we travel in a day, . . .[13]

On the morning of 18 May, Brigham Young called the captains of tens to his wagons, and gave them a severe lecture.

Clayton:

He referred to some who had left meat on the ground and would not use it because it was not hind quarter. Some would murmur because a fore quarter of meat was alloted to them, etc., which is not right, for God has given us a commandment that we should not waste meat, nor take life unless it is needful, but he can see a disposition in this camp to slaughter everything before them, yea if all the buffalo and game there is on our route were brought together to the camp, there are some who would never cease until they had destroyed the whole. Some men will shoot as much as thirty times at a rabbit if they did not kill it, and are continually wasting their ammunition, but when they have used all they have got, they may have the pleasure of carrying their empty guns to the mountains and back, for he will not furnish them. We have now meat enough to last some time if we will take proper care of it. As to the horsemen, there are none with the exception of Brothers Kimball, Woodruff, and Benson, that ever take the trouble to look out a good road for the wagons but all they seem to care about is to wait till their breakfast is cooked for them, and when they have eaten it, they mount their horses and scatter away, and if an antelope comes across the track, the whole of us must be stopped perhaps half an hour while they try to creep up near enough to kill it, but when we come to a bad place on the route, all the interest they have is to get across the best they can and leave myself and one or two others to pick out a crossing place and guide the camp all the time. Such things are not right, and he wants them to cease and all take an interest in the welfare of the camp, be united, and receive the meat as a blessing from God and not as a stink offering from the devil. It is not necessary to preach to the elders in this camp, they know what is right as well as he does, and he will not preach to them all the time. Let the captains do the best they know how and teach their men to do likewise.[13]

Two days before, machinery had been completed to measure accurately the distance travelled:

About noon today Brother Appleton Harmon completed the machinery on the wagon called a 'roadometer' by adding a wheel to revolve once in ten miles, showing each mile and also each quarter mile we travel, and then casing the whole over so as to secure it from the weather.[13]

On 22 May Clayton took a telescope to the top of a high bluff:

On the highest point I sat down and took a view of the surrounding country which is magnificent indeed. On the south at the distance of two miles from the river, there is a range of cedar trees on the bluffs which very much resemble some of the parks and seats of gentry in England. East I could see where we camped last night, the high grass still burning. Northeast, north, and northwest, alternately, appeared high swelling bluffs and valleys as far as the eye could see or the glass magnify. West, the course of the Platte for ten or fifteen miles and at about four or five miles distance, a large bend to the north brings it in contact with the bluffs on this side. At the distance, I should judge of about twenty miles, I could see Chimney Rock very plainly with the naked eye, which from here very much resembles the large factory chimneys in England, although I could not see the form of its base.[13]

On Saturday, 29 May, after the teams had been harnessed in the morning, Brigham Young preached a sermon to the company. He admonished:

'You never read of gambling, playing cards, checkers, dominoes, etc. in the scriptures, but you do read of men praising the Lord in the dance, but who ever read of praising the Lord in a game at cards? If any man had sense enough to play a game at cards, or dance a little without wanting to keep it up all the time, but exercise a little and then quit it and think no more of it, it would do well enough, but you want to keep it up till midnight and every night, and all the time. You don't know how to control your senses. . . . Do we suppose that we are going to look out a home for the Saints, a resting place, a place of peace where they can build up the kingdom and bid the nations welcome, with a low, mean, dirty, trifling, covetous, wicked spirit dwelling in our bosoms? It is vain! vain! Some of you are very fond of passing jokes, and will carry your jokes very far. But will you take a joke? If you do not want to take a joke, don't give a joke to your brethren. Joking, nonsense, profane language, trifling conversation and loud laughter do not belong to us. . . . I am one of the last to ask my brethren to enter into solemn covenants, but if they will not enter into a covenant to put away their iniquity and turn to the Lord and serve Him and acknowledge and honor His name, I want them to take their wagons and retreat back, for I shall go no farther under such a state of things. If we don't repent and quit our wickedness we will have more hinderances than we have had, and worse storms to encounter. . . .[13]

There were other, non-Mormon companies on the trail. On reaching the Sweetwater River, Clayton observed:

There is one of the gentile companies camped about a mile below, making the third company we have passed lately and it is the intention to keep ahead of them and have the advantage of the good feed and camping grounds.[13]

Clayton, 26 June:

Elder Pratt has gone ahead with the barometer to try to find the culminating point or highest dividing ridge of the South Pass as we are evidently at the east foot of the pass. Frémont represents that he did not discover the highest point on account of the ascent being so gradual that they were beyond it before they were aware of it, although in company with a man who has traveled it back and forth for seventeen years.[13]

An old trapper called Harris was the first of several men the Mormons met who advised against settlement in the region of Salt Lake.

Clayton:

Mr. Harris says he is well acquainted with the Bear River valley and the region around the Salt Lake. From his description, which is very discouraging, we have little chance to hope for a moderately good country anywhere in those regions. He speaks of the whole region as being sandy and destitute of timber and vegetation except the wild sage.[13]

Jim Bridger was another experienced mountain man they met who advised against settlement in Salt Lake Valley.

On 30 June the Mormons crossed the Green River on rafts, and reached Fort Bridger on 7 July. They continued their journey on the morning of the 9th. Next day a man called Miles Goodyear came into the Mormons' camp. He was making a farm in the Bear River valley, about seventy-five miles away from the camp. He recommended the valley for settlement, but the Mormons suspected he wanted them to make a road to his solitary farm for selfish motives.

There was snow on the ground, and it was bitterly cold at night. Clayton wrote in his journal on 11 July:

Morning fine with ice a quarter of an inch thick on the water pails. Walked on the mountain east with President Young and Kimball, from whence we had a pleasing view of the surrounding valley which is about ten miles wide. Abundance of timber on the mountains south and southwest and beyond that plenty of snow.... Porter, Brother Little, and others have been out with Goodyear to view the route he wishes us to take. They represent it as being bad enough, but we are satisfied it leads too far out of our course to be tempted to try it. There are some in camp who are getting discouraged about the looks of the country but thinking minds are not much disappointed, and we have no doubt of finding a place where the Saints can live which is all we ought to ask or expect.[13]

12 July:

Four and three-quarters of a mile beyond Bear River, passed a small spring of good clear cold water. At 11:50 halted for noon in the same narrow bottom near a ridge of high, rough rocks to the right, having traveled nine and three-quarters miles. There is scarcely any wagon track to be seen, only a few wagons of Hasting's [*sic*] company having come this route; ... President Young was taken very sick awhile before we halted. After resting two hours the camp moved on again, except President Young and Kimball's wagons, who concluded to remain there today on account of the President's sickness. ...

Tuesday, 13th. Awhile before noon, Elder Kimball and Howard Egan arrived from the company back. A meeting was called but suddenly dispersed by a thunder shower. After the rain ceased, Elder Kimball proposed that a company start from the camp with Elder Pratt to proceed to the Weber River canyon and ascertain if we can pass through safely, if not, to try and find a pass over the mountains. He reported that President Young is a little better this morning, but last evening was insensible and raving. Colonel Rockwood is also very sick and quite deranged. A company of twenty-two wagons, mostly ox teams, started on soon after dinner, in company with Elder Pratt, . . .

Thursday, 15th. . . . At twelve o'clock President Young, Kimball and all the rear wagons arrived, eight in number. The President is much better. Brother Rockwood is considerably better. . . .

Friday, 16th. . . . At a quarter to seven we formed our encampment, having traveled this afternoon nine and a half miles, and during the day sixteen and a quarter. We are yet enclosed by high mountains on each side, and this is the first good camping place we have seen since noon, not for lack of grass or water, but on account of the narrow gap between the mountains. Grass is pretty plentiful most of the distance and seems to grows higher the farther we go west. At this place the grass is about six feet high, and on the creek eight or ten feet high. There is one kind of grass which bears a head almost like wheat and grows pretty high, some of it six feet. There is a very singular echo in this ravine, the rattling of wagons resembles carpenters hammering at boards inside the highest rocks. The report of a rifle resembles a sharp crack of thunder and echoes from rock to rock for some time. The lowing of cattle and braying of mules seem to be answered beyond the mountains. Music, especially brass instruments, have a very pleasing effect and resemble a person standing inside the rock imitating every note. The echo, the high rocks on the north, high mountains on the south with the narrow ravine for a road, form a scenery at once romantic and more interesting than I have ever witnessed.[13]

Clayton's birthday fell the next day.

Arose to behold a fine pleasant morning, my health much better.

This is my thirty-third birthday. My mind naturally reverts back to my family and my heart is filled with blessings on their heads more than my tongue is able to express. . . . The cattle and mules seem very uneasy and continue lowing and braying all the morning. I suppose it is in consequence of the singular echoes, they no doubt thinking they are answered by others over the mountains. At 9:40 the camp renewed the journey and one mile farther arrived at the Red fork of the Weber River. We also seem to have a wide space to travel through and now turn to the right in a western course, the ravine having run mostly southwest. . . .

Sunday, 18th. This morning the camp was called together and addressed by Elder Kimball. He reports President Young as being a very sick man. He proposed to the brethren that . . . they should meet together and pray and exhort each other that the Lord may turn away sickness from our midst and from our President that we may proceed on our journey. . . .

Monday, 19th. . . . President Young considerably better. At 7:45 we started onward leaving President Young and Kimball's wagons and several others. We found the road very rough on account of loose rocks and cobble stones. After traveling two and a quarter miles, we forded the river and found it about eighteen inches deep but proceeded without difficulty. . . . Three-quarters of a mile from the ford we found the place to make the cutoff and there halted awhile. I put a guide board up at this place marked as follows: 'Pratt's Pass to avoid canyon. To Fort Bridger 74¼ miles.' Brother Pack, having charge of the company, concluded to move on slowly and be making our way up the mountains. We accordingly started and after traveling a mile from the forks began to ascend and wind around the mountains. We found the road exceedingly rough and crooked and very dangerous on wagons. . . . The descent is not very steep but exceedingly dangerous to wagons being mostly on the side hill over large cobble stones, causing the wagons to slide very badly. . . . Several accidents have happened to wagons today . . .

Wednesday, 21st. . . . Orson Pratt's company are camped a half a mile ahead of us . . . The cannon is left back on the other side of the mountains. . . .

Thursday, 22nd. ... [*we*] soon came up with Elder Pratt's company. There were several bad places in the road where the brethren spent considerable time fixing them. ... It is evident that the emigrants who passed this way last year must have spent a great deal of time cutting a road through the thickly set timber and heavy brush wood. ... After traveling one and three-quarters miles, we found the road crossing the creek again to the north side and then ascending up a very steep, high hill. It is so very steep as to be almost impossible for heavy wagons to ascend and so narrow that the least accident might precipitate a wagon down a bank three or four hundred feet, – in which case it would certainly be dashed to pieces. Colonel Markham and another man went over the hill and returned up the canyon to see if a road cannot be cut through and avoid this hill. While passing up, a bear started near them but soon was out of sight amongst the very high grass. Brother Markham says a good road can soon be made down the canyon by digging a little and cutting through the bushes some ten or fifteen rods. A number of men went to work immediately to make the road which will be much better than to attempt crossing the hill and will be sooner done.

Agreeable to President Young's instructions, Elder Pratt accompanied by George A. Smith, John Brown, Joseph Mathews, John Pack, O. P. Rockwell and J. C. Little started on this morning on horses to seek out a suitable place to plant some potatoes, turnips, etc., so as to preserve the seed at least.[13]

On 20 July, Orson Pratt and Erastus Snow, who joined the advance party, climbed a hill to avoid a canyon through which a creek dashed wildly, and suddenly came upon a view of the Great Salt Lake and valley. Here is Snow's account of an historic moment in the history of Utah :

The thicket down the narrows, at the mouth of the canyon, was so dense that we could not penetrate through it. I crawled for some distance on my hands and knees through this thicket, until I was compelled to return, admonished to by the rattle of a snake which lay coiled up under my nose, having almost put my hand on him; but as he gave me the friendly warning, I thanked him and retreated. We raised on to a high point south of the narrows, where we got a view of

the Great Salt Lake in this valley, and each of us, without saying a
word to the other, instinctively, as if by inspiration, raised our hats
from our heads, and then, swinging our hats, shouted: 'Hosannah to
God and the Lamb!' We could see the canes down in the valley, on
what is now called Mill Creek, which looked like inviting grain, and
thitherward we directed our course.[40]

*By the time Brigham Young reached the valley about six acres of
potatoes and other vegetables had already been planted. Other companies of Mormons went westward to Salt Lake Valley in the following
months: thousands of men, women, and children, with horses, oxen,
cows, sheep, hogs, and chickens. Young returned east on 26 August,
meeting on the way companies of Mormons moving westward. Others
spent the winter of 1846/47 in camps at Council Bluffs and elsewhere.
In the spring of 1848 Brigham Young arranged the migration of
most Mormons remaining in Missouri. Saints also came to Salt
Lake Valley from Europe.*

Land could be purchased for five shillings an acre. The Millennial
Star, *the Mormons' journal in Britain, in the issue of 1 February 1848,
announced ecstatically:*

The channel of Saints' emigration to the land of Zion is now
opened. The resting place of Israel for the last days has been
discovered. In the elevated valley of the Salt and Utah Lakes, with
the beautiful river Jordan running through it, is the newly established
Stake of Zion. There vegetation flourishes with magic rapidity. And
the food of man, or staff of life, leaps into maturity from the
bowels of Mother Earth with astonishing celerity.[33]

*Clouds of crickets and grasshoppers attacked the first crops. When
the plague was at its height flocks of gulls descended to devour the
insects. Frémont, and others, had reported seeing large numbers of gulls
at Salt Lake: but to the settlers it seemed divine intervention.*

*Grain was successfully grown and ripened that first summer. On
10 August a harvest festival was held at Salt Lake City, in the bowery
at the centre of the fort the Mormons had built, when, to quote Pratt,
'large sheaves of wheat, rye, barley, oats, and other productions were
hoisted on poles for public exhibition'.*

In March 1848 the city had a population of 1,671, with 423 houses erected. Because of lack of timber these early dwellings were built of adobe clay. Inexperience in handling the clay led to several homes collapsing about their occupants once they met with rains and frosts. Some families had to lodge in their wagons. House furniture was of the most primitive kind. Brigham Young himself led the largest company to cross the plains in '48, reaching Salt Lake City in September. By the winter of '48 the population of the city had risen to about five thousand persons. And the Saints had already set up three sawmills, one flour mill, and a threshing machine run by water. Another sawmill and a flour mill were nearly completed, and also mills for the manufacture of sugar from corn stalks. The winter was severe, with snow from 1 December to late in February, and the temperature often dropping below zero. But the Saints held on, and a boost to their prosperity was about to come from an unexpected source.

The Mormons had moved westward with God, but now the quest for gold was to bring a flood of travellers pouring across the plains during the spring, summer, and autumn of '49. Most of them followed the by now much described California Trail. And Salt Lake City was ideally situated to provide the gold seekers with a stopping place for recruitment.

Westward for Gold:
The Gold Rush,
1848/9

The discovery of gold in California is credited to James W. Marshall, a carpenter by trade, with his employer, General John Sutter, of Sutter's Fort, being closely concerned. Ironically, neither man prospered from the find.

Marshall, a taciturn, independent wanderer, had rode, alone and carrying the tools of his trade, from Fort Leavenworth to Oregon in 1844, moving south to California in the following year. Sutter employed him as head carpenter. In the spring of '47, when he was thirty-six years old, Marshall proposed to his boss a project for setting up a sawmill in the mountains from which lumber could be floated down river to the fort. Sutter agreed, promising Marshall a partnership in the venture. Marshall's explorations led him to choose a site for the mill at Coloma, on a bend in the American River. It was here, in January 1848, as the river was being dammed and the mill constructed, that Marshall found gold. An account by Marshall of the discovery was published in Hutchings' California Magazine, *November 1857.*

While we were in the habit at night of turning the water through the tail race we had dug for the purpose of widening and deepening the race, I used to go down in the morning to see what had been done by the water through the night; and about half past seven o'clock on or about the 19th of January – I am not quite certain to a day, but it was between the 18th and 20th of that month – 1848, I went down as usual, and after shutting off the water from the race I stepped into it, near the lower end, and there, upon the rock, about six inches beneath the surface of the water, I DISCOVERED THE GOLD. I was entirely alone at the time. I picked up one or two pieces and examined them attentively; and having some general knowledge of minerals, I could not call to mind more than two which in any way resembled this – *sulphuret of iron*, very bright and brittle; and *gold*, bright, yet malleable; I then tried it between two rocks, and found that it could be beaten into a different shape, but not broken. I then collected four or five pieces and went up to Mr. Scott (who was working at the carpenter's bench making the mill wheel) with the pieces in my hand, and said, 'I have found it.'

'What is it?' inquired Scott.

'Gold,' I answered.

'Oh! no,' returned Scott, 'that can't be.'

I replied positively, – 'I know it to be nothing else.' . . .

Four days afterwards I went to the Fort for provisions, and carried with me about three ounces of the gold, . . .[30]

According to John Sutter:

It was a rainy afternoon when Mr. Marshall arrived at my office in the Fort, very wet. I was somewhat surprised to see him, as he was down a few days previous; and when, I sent up to Coloma a number of teams with provisions, mill irons, etc., etc. He told me then that he had some important and interesting news which he wished to communicate secretly to me, and wished me to go with him to a place where we should not be disturbed, and where no listeners could come and hear what we had to say. I went with him to my private rooms; he requested me to lock the door; I complied, but I told him at the same time that nobody was in the house except the clerk, who was in his office in a different part of the house; after requesting of me something which he wanted, which my servants brought and then left the room, I forgot to lock the doors, and it happened that the door was opened by the clerk just at the moment when Marshall took a rag from his pocket, showing me the yellow metal: he had about two ounces of it; but how quick Mr. M. put the yellow metal in his pocket again can hardly be described. The clerk came to see me on business, and excused himself for interrupting me, and as soon as he had left I was told, 'now lock the doors; didn't I tell you that we might have listeners?' I told him that he need fear nothing about that, as it was not the habit of this gentleman; but I could hardly convince him that he need not to be suspicious. Then Mr. M. began to show me this metal, which consisted of small pieces and specimens, some of them worth a few dollars; he told me that he had expressed his opinion to the laborers at the mill, that this might be gold; but some of them were laughing at him and called him

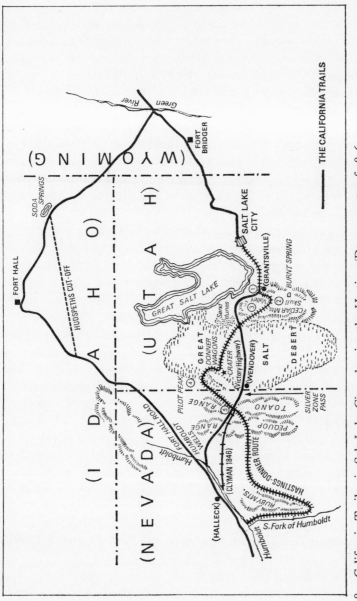

8. California Trails via Salt Lake City, showing the Hastings/Donner route of 1846

a crazy man, and could not believe such a thing. After having proved the metal with aqua fortis, which I found in my apothecary shop, likewise with other experiments, and read the long article 'gold' in the Encyclopedia Americana I declared this to be gold of the finest quality, of at least 23 carats. . . . [41]

The following day Sutter rode fifty-four miles to the sawmill.

I went in the race and picked up several pieces of this gold, several of the laborers gave me some which they had picked up, and from Marshall I received a part. I told them that I would get a ring made of this gold as soon as it could be done in California; and I have a heavy ring made, with my family's coat of arms engraved on the outside, and on the inside of the ring is engraved, 'The first gold, discovered in January, 1848.'[41]

As soon as the sawmill at Coloma was completed, the workers resigned to mine gold (which they had already been doing in their spare time). Then, for the same motive, Sutter's employees at his flour mill and tannery also resigned. Even his Indian workers quit. Thereafter Sutter's mercantile fortunes declined. And Marshall, who had first discovered the gold, did not share in the subsequent bonanza.

Sam Brennan, who had brought a shipload of Mormons to California in '46, is said to have started the stampede to the diggings from San Francisco, when early in May of '48 he rode through the streets shouting excitedly: 'Gold! Gold! Gold! Gold from the American River!' The effect was dramatic. Doctors, lawyers, hotel owners, storekeepers, tradesmen of every description – each abandoned his practice or business to take to the mountains, having first procured any container – bowl, tray, warming pan – that would hold sand and water. Schoolchildren were left without teachers. The two newspapers had to close down. Farmers quit their ranches. Within a month three-quarters of the houses in the town were deserted. Ships in the harbour were deserted by their crews. Soldiers of the American Army of Occupation followed the lead of the sailors, and for a time the Military Governor of California had to cook his own meals.

Gold fever spread to other Californian settlements. The Rev. Walter Colton, Alcalde at Monterey, tells of its arrival there on 20 June:

My messenger . . . has returned with specimens of the gold; he dismounted in a sea of upturned faces. As he drew forth the yellow lumps from his pockets, and passed them around among the eager crowd, the doubts, which had lingered till now, fled. . . . The excitement produced was intense; and many were soon busy in their hasty preparations for a departure to the mines. The family who had kept house for me caught the moving infection. Husband and wife were both packing up; the blacksmith dropped his hammer, the carpenter his plane, the mason his trowel, the farmer his sickle, the baker his loaf, and the tapster his bottle. All were off for the mines, . . .[15]

In 1848 news could take a long time to travel two thousand miles, and by the time the Americans in the eastern states had been injected with gold fever the winter was on its way and had to be suffered to pass before the overland trip to the California diggings could be undertaken in the spring of '49.

The fever was spread in great measure by no less a person than President Polk. In June '48 Colonel R. B. Mason, the Military Governor of California, visited some of the 'lower mines' and reported what he saw to Washington.

The hill sides were thickly strewn with canvas tents and bush arbours; a store was erected, and several boarding shanties in operation. The day was intensely hot, yet about two hundred men were at work in the full glare of the sun, washing for gold – some with tin pans, some with close woven Indian baskets, but the greater part had a rude machine, known as the cradle.

This is on rockers, six or eight feet long, open at the foot, and at its head has a coarse grate or sieve; the bottom is rounded, with small cleats nailed across. Four men are required to work this machine; one digs the ground in the bank close by the stream; another carries it to the cradle and empties it on the grate; a third gives a violent rocking motion to the machine; whilst a fourth dashes on water from the stream itself. The sieve keeps the coarse stones from entering the cradle, the current of water washes off the earthy matter, and the gravel is gradually carried out at the foot of the machine, leaving the gold mixed with a heavy fine black sand above the first cleats.

The sand and gold mixed together are then drawn off through augur holes into a pan below, are dried in the sun, and afterwards separated by blowing off the sand. . . . The gold in the lower mines is in fine bright scales, of which I send several specimens.[31]

President Polk had the gold Colonel Mason sent displayed at the War Office, and in his annual message to Congress delivered on 5 December 1848 helped spread gold fever in the east:

It was known that mines of the precious metals existed to a considerable extent in California at the time of its acquisition. Recent discoveries render it probable that these mines are more extensive and valuable than was anticipated. The accounts of the abundance of gold in that territory are of such an extraordinary character as would scarcely command belief, were they not corroborated by the authentic reports of officers in the public service, who have visited the mineral district. . . .[37]

California had become officially part of the United States a few days after James Marshall found gold in the American River. The Mexican War, which began in May 1846, after a clash on the Rio Grande, led to the United States acquiring upper California, ceded by the Mexicans in signing the Treaty of Guadalupe Hidalgo on 2 February 1848.

Even so, the number of Americans entering California in '48 was light; but news of the gold diggings, their riches confirmed by the President himself, brought a rush of 'forty-niners' from the eastern states. The first persons to set out went by sea, round Cape Horn, a journey of seventeen thousand miles in overcrowded, often unseaworthy vessels. The crews deserted at San Francisco to join the gold-seekers. Others took a sea-land-sea route: crossing the humid, unhealthy Isthmus of Panama and completing the journey by ship along the Pacific coast. But the great majority followed the overland route pioneered by John Bidwell and others. Newspapers carried maps and advice as to what equipment should be taken to California. They published exaggerated reports of huge fortunes made in a few weeks. The Washington Globe, *13 March, reported a lecture by a Mr Atherton:*

The reports concerning the gold mines were not exaggerated in the newspapers; that the supply of gold was absolutely inexhaustible; and that, in his opinion, *one hundred thousand persons* could not exhaust it in *ten or twelve years*. The gains of miners varied from one ounce to one thousand dollars per day. Mr. Atherton said that the largest lump of gold he ever saw was seven pounds weight; it was assayed, and found to be 19¾ carats fine. He also saw it stated, a few days before he left San Francisco, that one man had got 12,000 dollars in six days. Another had obtained 36 pounds in one day. Of the truth of this story he had no more doubt than he had of his own existence. He said that the gold region was as large as New York State, and that a hundred thousand persons would be only two to the square mile. One handful, he said, of the earth where gold is found yields half an ounce of pure gold, on an average.[3]

No wonder that never before had such numbers, nor such a strange gallimaufry of people, set out west from the frontier towns. Some were going for reasons similar to the emigrants of earlier years: to try their luck in trade or farming, or to fulfil an urge for adventure. But their numbers were tiny beside the throng who were being driven two thousand miles by visions of gold.

William Kelly, an Irish journalist, went to observe and to write about what he saw. He reached St Louis in the early spring, and wrote:

. . . the further west I proceeded, the more intense became the Californian fever. California met you here at every turn, every corner, every dead wall; every post and pillar was labelled with Californian placards. The shops seemed to contain nothing but articles for California. As you proceeded along the flagways, you required great circumspection, lest your coat-tails should be whisked into some of the multifarious Californian gold-washing machines, kept in perpetual motion by little ebony cherubs, singing

> *Oh, Susannah, don't you cry for me,*
> *I'm gone to California with my wash-bowl on my knee.*

Californian advertisements, and extracts from Californian letters, filled all the newspapers; and 'are you for California?' was the constantly recurring question of the day; so that one would almost imagine the whole city was on wheels bound for that attractive region.[25]

Fur-trappers and mountain men, and men who had already made the overland trip to California, turned up on the frontier to act as guides

to companies. One estimate put the number of persons on the California
Trail in '49 at fifty thousand. Some went by wagon, some on horseback,
some even on foot. Never before had so many 'greenhorns' taken to the
plains. Some had bought wagons and animals in such poor condition that
neither could possibly survive the journey. Some overloaded their
wagons with tables, chests of drawers, double beds, and other heavy
articles of furniture that had to be jettisoned along the trail. Many
were to die on the journey.

But thoughts of gold and the animation of so large an assemblage of
people generated a reckless excitement, even gaiety, among the emigrants.
Something of this care-free if naïve spirit is conveyed by some verse from
the trail journal of J. Goldsborough Bruff (his prose was of better
standard):

> Hurrah for a trip o'er the plains,
>   With wagons and steers and mules;
> No matter for clouds and rains,
>   'Go ahead' is the order that rules!
>
> Swallow your coffee and hitch up,
>   Drop your fried bacon and fritters,
> Straddle your saddles and switch up
>   Roll ahead quick with your critters.
>
> Here we go, trav'ling for Sun set,
>   And leaving the east in the rear;—
> I'll warrant we'll have some fun yet—
>   Shouldn't wonder if t'was very near—
>
> The hour for your camping has come,
>   Roll, form a corral with your waggons
> Your beasts picket so they can't roam
>   Get out your bacon and flaggons,
> Consider yourselves, boys, at home.
>
> Come bring in your asses and steers,
>   And quick put some sentinels out,
> And lay in your tents without fears,
>   No red skins are seen round about.[8]

The St Joseph Adventure *reported that by 18 May 2,850 wagons had crossed the river at St Joseph, and 1,500 elsewhere.*

The Indians on the plains were appalled by the flood of white people moving westward across their territory, causing a depletion of buffaloes, by shooting them, chasing them out of the territory, and denuding the region of their food. Sarah Royce, who was travelling with her husband and two-year-old daughter, tells how one group of Indians asked for monetary compensation from each member of their company:

. . . Indians, by hundreds; and soon they had ranged themselves along on each side of the way. A group of them came forward, and at the Captain's command our company halted, while he with several others went to meet the Indians and hold a parley. It turned out that they had gathered to demand the payment of a certain sum per head for every emigrant passing through this part of the country, which they claimed as their own. The men of our company after consultation, resolved that the demand was unreasonable! that the country we were traveling over belonged to the United States, and that these red men had no right to stop us. The Indians were then plainly informed that the company meant to proceed at once without paying a dollar. That if unmolested, they would not harm anything; but if the Indians attempted to stop them, they would open fire with all their rifles and revolvers. At the Captain's word of command all the men of the company then armed themselves with every weapon to be found in their wagons. Revolvers, knives, hatchets, glittered in their belts; rifles and guns bristled on their shoulders. The drivers raised aloft their long whips, the rousing words 'Go 'long Buck' – 'Bright!' – 'Dan!' were given all along the line, and we were at once moving between long but not very compact rows of half-naked redskins; many of them well armed; others carrying but indifferent weapons; while all wore in their faces the expression of sullen disappointment, mingled with a half-defiant scowl, that suggested the thought of future night attacks, when darkness and thickets should give them greater advantage. For the present, however, they had evidently made up their minds to let us pass, and we soon lost sight of them.[39]

Sarah Royce goes on:

But another enemy, unseen, and without one audible word of

demand or threat, was in that very hour advancing upon us, and made our wagon his first point of attack. The oldest of the men who had joined company with my husband, complained of intense pain and sickness, and was soon obliged to lie down in the wagon, which, being large, gave room for quite a comfortable bed behind the seat where Mary and I sat. Soon, terrible spasms convulsed him; the Captain was called, examined the case, and ordered a halt. Medicine was administered which afforded some relief. About this time a horseman or two appeared, with the intelligence that some companies in advance of us were camped at the ford of the Elkhorn River, not more than two miles distant, and that there was a physician among them. We therefore made the sick man as comfortable as we could, and went on. Arrived at the encampment the Doctor pronounced the disease Asiatic Cholera. Everything was done that could be under the circumstances, but nothing availed, and in two or three hours the poor old man expired.

The most prompt and energetic sympathy was shown by our fellow travelers. The fact was at once recognized that close contact with the disease for several hours had exposed us to contagion, and had also made necessary the disinfecting of our wagon and all it contained. There were in the encampment those who had tents as well as wagons, and soon a comfortable tent, with a cot bed and other conveniences, was placed at our disposal till our things could be disinfected. That Sunday night was one never to be forgotten by me. I positively refused to lie down, because there was room and covering for only one besides Mary – my husband had been on guard the night before, and on most exhausting duty all day; so I insisted upon his resting, while I sat by my little one, leaning my head on her pillow, and tried to sleep.

But a storm began in the evening. The wind moaned fitfully, and rain fell constantly. I could not sleep. I rose and walked softly to the tent door, put the curtains aside and looked out. The body of the dead man lay stretched upon a rudely constructed bier beside our wagon a few rods off, the sheet that was stretched over it flapped in the wind with a sound that suggested the idea of some vindictive creature struggling restlessly in bonds; while its white flutterings, dimly seen, confirmed the ghastly fancy. Not many yards beyond, a party of Indians – who had, for a day or two, been playing the part of friendly hangers-on to one of the large companies – had raised a rude skin tent and built a fire, round which they were seated on the ground, – looking unearthly in its flickering light, and chanting, hour after hour, a wild melancholy chant, varied by occasional high, shrill notes as of distressful appeal. The minor key ran through it all. I knew it was a death dirge.

Morning came at last. In the early dawn the body of the old man was laid in the grave that had been dug in a hill-side nearby. Then came the work of cleansing the wagon, washing bed clothes, and thoroughly sunning and airing everything; . . .[39]

There had been cases of cholera on the frontier, mainly at Independence, before the emigrants set out. It was present along the trail to a hundred miles beyond Fort Laramie and appeared again, inexplicably, at the Humboldt Sink.

An eye-witness, the Hon. F. A. Chenoweth, recalled:

Very soon after the assembled throng took up its march over the plains the terrible wave of cholera struck them in a way to carry the utmost terror and dismay into all parts of the moving mass. The number of the fatally stricken after the smoke and dust were cleared away was not numerically so frightful as appeared to those who were in the midst of it. But the name of *cholera* in a multitude – unorganized and un-numbered – is like a leak in the bottom of a ship whose decks are thronged with passengers. . . . This terrible malady seemed to spend its most deadly force on the flat prairie east of and about Fort Laramie.

One of the appalling effects of this disease was to cause the most devoted friends to desert, in case of attack, the fallen one. Many a stout and powerful man fought the last battle alone upon the prairie. When the rough hand of the cholera was laid upon families they rarely had either the assistance or the sympathy of their neighbors or traveling companions.

There was one feature mixed with all this terror that afforded some degree of relief, and that was that there was no case of lingering suffering. When attacked, a single day ordinarily ended the strife in death or recovery. A vast amount of wagons, with beds and blankets, were left by the roadside, [which] no man, not even an Indian, would approach or touch through fear of the unknown, unseen destroyer.

While there were sad instances of comrades deserting comrades in this hour of extreme trial, I can not pass this point of my story without stating that there were many instances of heroic devotion to the sick, when such attention was regarded as almost equivalent to the offering up of the well and healthy for the mere hope of saving the sick and dying.[12]

J. Goldsborough Bruff, who was with a company of sixty-six persons with sixteen wagons from Washington, kept a detailed journal that included each grave marking he observed along the trail. Between 2 July and 8 August, from approaching Chimney Rock to reaching Green River, he recorded forty-four graves, including:

Jno. Hoover, died June 18. 49
Aged 12 years. Rest in peace,
Sweet boy, for thy travels are over

Wm. K. Colly, of Ray Co. Mo.
Died of Cholera, June 18.
1849, Aged 49 years.
Has 1 brother in Company.

Jno. Campbell,
of Layfayette Co. Mo.
came to his death by the
accidental discharge
of his gun, while riding
with a friend, June 21.
1849. Aged 18 years.

Alex. M. Brown
Died June 23 '49
of Louisville, Kty
of Chronic Diarohea
aged 22 years 5 months and 4 days.
on foot – Recently of Metropolis Ill.

Adison Laughlin
died July 2nd '49.
A member of the Spartan
Band, organized at
Trader's Point,
aged 19 years.

Robert Gilmore
and wife,
Died of cholera,
July 18th, 1849.[8]

On 8 July Bruff's own company added one more to the trail graves:
At 1 p.m. poor Bishop died, of Cholera. – The first casualty in the
Company, sudden and astounding, was this very mysterious and
fatal visitation. Yesterday, in presence of the diseased, I remarked
how very fortunate we had been, in all respect[s], and trusted we
might continue so. The messmates of the deceased laid him out,
sewed him up in his blue blanket, and prepared a bier, formed of his
tent-poles. I had a grave dug in a neighbouring ridge, on left of the
trail, about 400 yards from it. Dry clay and gravel, and coarse white
sandstone on the next hill, afforded slabs to line it with, making a
perfect vault. I sat 3 hours in the hot sun, and sculptured a head and
foot stone; and filled the letters with blacking from the hub of a wheel.

I then organized a funeral procession, men all in clean clothes and
uniforms, with music, (a key-bugle, flute, violin and accordian) and
two and two, with the Stars & stripes over the body, we marched
to the measured time of the dirge, deposited the body of our comrade
in the grave, an elderly gentleman read the burial service, and we
filled up the grave, erected the stones, and returned to camp. . . .[8]

As Alonzo Delano was crossing the South Pass on 28 June, an express
rider passed . . .

. . . who told us that there was an immense throng behind, and that
at least a thousand wagons were detained at the South Platte, on
account of a sudden rise of the river, which prevented fording. He
informed us that there was a vast amount of sickness and suffering

among them; the grass was consumed, and many of the cattle had perished for want of food. To us their prospect seemed cheerless enough, for a great part of the way along the North Fork, and up to our present advance, the grass barely afforded sustenance to the trains already passed, and we were sometimes compelled to pass two miles out of the road to find forage. None would be left when they came along. . . .[16]

Soon after setting out west, large trains broke up into smaller units. Delano :

On leaving the Missouri, nearly every train was an organized company, with general regulations for mutual safety, and with a captain chosen by themselves, as a nominal head. On reaching the South Pass, we found that the great majority had either divided, broken up entirely, making independent and helter-skelter marches towards California. Some had divided from policy, because they were too large, and on account of the difficulty of procuring grass in one place for so many cattle, while others, disgusted by the overbearing propensities of some men, would not endure it, and others still, from mutual ill-feelings and disagreements among themselves. Small parties of twenty men got along decidedly the best; and three men to a mess, or wagon, is sufficient for safety as well as harmony.[16]

When Delano reached Green River on 3 July, he found that . . .

The whole plain was covered with tents, wagons and men, and there were also a detachment of troops, on their way to Oregon, under the command of Major Simonton, who were stopping a few days to rest and recruit the strength of their animals.[16]

The emigrants had to register with a ferryman to arrange a crossing, for which there was a two to three days' delay, so great was the number of wagons.

While Delano was at the Green River encampment, a man called Brown killed another by stabbing him in the back with a knife.

A meeting of emigrants was called, and General Allen, from Lewis county, Missouri, was called to the chair, when the atrocious deed was set forth, and it was determined by a series of resolutions to arrest the villain, give him a fair trial, and if found guilty, to execute him on the spot. Major Simonton seconded the views of the emigrants, in order to protect them against similar assassinations. In addition to a dozen athletic volunteers, who stood forth at the call, he detailed a file of soldiers to assist in the capture of the murderer. Several murders had been committed on the road, and all felt the necessity of doing something to protect themselves, where there was no other law but brute force.[16]

Next day, 4 July, the volunteers returned without having captured Brown, but bringing with them a man called Williams, who on 23 June, in camp at the Devil's Gate, an unusual chasm which the Sweetwater River passed through, had shot and killed a man who had been threatening for some time to kill Williams. Williams agreed to stand trial before a Green River jury, and employed B. F. Washington, a young lawyer from Virginia, to defend him. Alonzo Delano watched the proceedings degenerate into farce:

General Allen elected chief justice, assisted by Major Simonton, who, with many of his officers, and a large crowd of emigrants, was present. A jury was empaneled, and court opened under a fine clump of willows. There, in that primitive court-house, on the bank of Green River, the first court was held in this God-forsaken land, for the trial of a man accused of the highest crime. At the commencement, as much order reigned as in any lawful tribunal of the States. But it was the 4th of July, and the officers and lawyers had been celebrating it to the full, and a spirit other than that of '76 was apparent.

Mr. Washington, a counsel for the defendant, arose, and in a somewhat lengthy and occasionally flighty speech, denied the right of the court to act in the case at all. This, as a matter of law, was true enough, but his remark touched the pride of the old commandant, who gave a short, pithy and *spirited* contradiction to some of the learned counsel's remarks. This elicited a *spirited* reply, until, spiritually speaking, the spirits of the speakers ceased to flow in the tranquil spirit of the commencement, and the spirit of contention waxed so fierce, that some of the officers' spirits led them to take up in Washington's defence. From taking up words, they finally proceeded to take up stools and other beligerent attitudes. Blows, in short, began to be exchanged, the cause of which would have puzzled a '*Philadelphia lawyer*' to determine, when the emigrants interfered to prevent a further ebullition of patriotic feeling, and words were recalled, hands shaken, a general amnesty proclaimed, and this spirited exhibition of law, patriotism '*vi et armis*', was consigned to the 'vasty deep'. Order and good feeling 'once more reigned in Denmark'. Williams, in the meantime, seeing that his affair had merged into something wholly irrelevant, with a sort of tacit consent, withdrew, for his innocence was generally understood, and no attempt was made to detain him. The sheriff did not even adjourn the court, and it may be in session to this day, for aught I know.[16]

Thousands of forty-niners took the Mormon Trail to Salt Lake City. Understandably, relations between Mormons and forty-niners were at first wary. The Saints were face to face with 'Gentiles' from areas in the east where the two peoples had clashed violently. And most forty-niners had imbibed stories of the strangeness and wickedness of Mormon belief and practice. But apprehension and mistrust melted away rapidly; for each party had much to gain in the circumstances from contact with the other.

Irish journalist William Kelly had started out from the frontier on 16 April, and his company must have been in the vanguard of those who took the Mormon Trail, for they had to show the Saints an Independence newspaper for 7 April before convincing them that they had indeed made the overland crossing and not wintered at Fort Laramie.

Kelly:

At first the city was not visible, but on passing over a piece of table-land, the new capital of the Mormons became revealed – not, I must admit, with any very striking effect, for it was too young as yet to boast the stately ornaments of spire and dome which first attract the eye of the anxious traveller. We saw from here with great distinctness the plan of the place, which had nothing novel or peculiar about it, laid out in very wide regular streets, radiating from a large space in the centre, where there appeared the basement and tall scaffolding-poles of an immense building in progress of erection. The houses were far apart, each being allotted a space for gardens and enclosure, which caused it to cover a very large space of ground.

We were soon discovered coming down the slope, and as we entered the precincts of the town the inhabitants came to the front of their houses, but showed no disposition to open an acquaintance account, believing us to be an exclusively American caravan. So soon, however, as they were undeceived, they came about us in great numbers, enquiring what we had to dispose of. They were neat and well clad, their children tidy, the rosy glow of health and robustness mantling on the cheeks of all, while the softer tints of female loveliness prevailed to a degree that goes far to prove those 'Latter-Day Saints' have very correct notions of angelic perfecta-bility. We politely declined several courteous offers of gratuitous lodging, selecting our quarters in a luxuriant meadow at the north end of the city; but had not our tents well pitched when we had loads of presents – butter, milk, small cheeses, eggs, and vegetables, which we received reluctantly, not having any equivalent returns to make, except in money, which they altogether declined; in fact, the only thing we had in superabundance were preserved apples and peaches, a portion of which we presented to one of the elders, who gave a delightful party in the evening, at which all our folk were present. We found a very large and joyous throng assembled; the house turned inside out to make more room on the occasion, with gaiety, unembarrassed by ceremony, animating the whole, making me almost fancy I was spending the evening amongst the crowded haunts of the old world, instead of a sequestered valley lying between the Utah and Timpanago mountains. After tea was served,

> *There were the sounds of dancing feet*
> *Mingling with the tones of music sweet;*

or, as Dermot MacFig would say,

> *We shook a loose toe,*
> *While he humoured the bow;*

keeping it up to a late hour, perfectly enraptured with the Mormon ladies, and Mormon hospitality.[25]

Kelly was surprised to discover polygamy in practice at Salt Lake City:

I was not aware, before, that polygamy was sanctioned by their creed, beyond a species of etherial platonism which accorded to its especial saints chosen partners called 'spiritual wives'; but I now found that these, contrary to one's ordinary notions of spiritualism, give birth to cherubs and unfledged angels. When our party arrived, we were introduced to a staid, matronly-looking lady as Mrs. ****; and as we proceeded up the room, to a blooming young creature, a fitting mother for a celestial progeny, as the other Mrs. ****, without any worldly or spiritual distinction whatsoever. . . .[25]

The Irish journalist was impressed by the neatness and cleanliness of Mormon homes; and by Mormon energy and productivity.

The houses are small, principally of brick, built up only as temporary abodes, until the more urgent and important matter of enclosure and cultivation are attended to; but I never saw anything to surpass the ingenuity of arrangement with which they are fitted up, and the scrupulous cleanliness with which they are kept. There were tradesmen and artisans of all descriptions, but no regular stores, or workshops, except forges. Still, from the shoeing of a waggon to the mending of a watch, there was no difficulty experienced in getting it done, as cheap and as well put out of hand as in any other city in America. Notwithstanding the oppressive temperature, they were all hard at work at their trades, and abroad in the fields weeding, moulding, and irrigating; and it certainly speaks volumes for their energy and industry, to see the quantity of land they have fenced in, and the breadth under cultivation, considering the very short time since they had founded the settlement in 1847. There was ample promise of an abundant harvest, in magnificent crops of wheat, maize, potatoes, and every description of garden vegetable, all of which require irrigation, as there is little or no rain in this region, a Salt Lake shower being estimated at a drop to each inhabitant. They have numerous herds of the finest cattle, droves of excellent sheep, with horses and mules enough and to spare, but very few pigs, persons having them being obliged to keep them chained, as the fences are not close enough to prevent them damaging the crops. However, they have legions of superior poultry, so that they live in the most plentiful manner possible. We exchanged and purchased some mules and horses on very favourable terms, knowing we would stand in need of strong teams in crossing the Sierra Nevada.[25]

Once the initial suspicion of each other had been broken, Mormons and emigrants traded to mutual advantage. The emigrants bought flour, milk, butter, and vegetables, and in turn carried mechanical equipment, tools, and merchandise useful to the Saints. Some of the Mormons who had gone to California in the ship chartered by Sam Brennan had turned up at Salt Lake City with bags of gold dust, the sight of which galvanized even the most trail-weary forty-niner. Emigrants offered heavy wagons in exchange for light ones. Some of the travellers who were carrying heavy machinery and miscellaneous merchandise with hopes of making a huge profit in California learned at Salt Lake City that ship-loads of similar articles were on the way to California via Cape Horn. They accordingly cut their losses and sold out to the Saints. If the Mormons did trade to great profit with the California-bound 'gentiles', they nevertheless showed hospitality and kindness in administering to the sick among the visitors, many of whom spent the winter in Salt Lake City.

But Brigham Young felt it necessary to issue an admonitory epistle : 'The true use of gold is for paving streets, covering houses, and making culinary dishes, and when the Saints shall have preached the gospel, raised grain, and built up cities enough, the Lord will open up the way for a supply of gold, to the perfect satisfaction of his people.' *The caution was prompted by a number of Mormons having succumbed to the temptation of joining the race to California.*

Sarah Royce, with husband and child, was grateful for Mormon hospitality at Salt Lake City. She informs:

At this point, company organizations were broken up, almost without exception, and every man proceeded to make such arrangements as seemed best to himself and those belonging to the same wagon. In many cases, even those owning teams and wagons together, sold out and parted goods, each taking his own way. [39]

It was tough on the trail for the single traveller, of which there were a surprising number. Alonzo Delano tells of two such men met separately in late July between Goose Creek and Humboldt Wells.

At night, a man came to our camp who had taken a passage at St.

Louis in the Pioneer line of spring wagons, which were advertised to go through in sixty days. He was on foot, armed with a knife and pistol, and carried in a small knapsack all his worldly goods, except a pair of blankets, which were rolled up on his shoulders. He told us that at Willow Springs their mules gave out, and there was a general distribution of property, a small proportion of the passengers only obtaining mules, the rest being obliged to go a thousand miles without supplies, in the best manner they could, trusting to luck and the emigrants for provisions. The passengers had each paid two hundred dollars for their passage, but now, like the Irishman on the towpath, were obliged to work it out. No emigrant would see him suffer under such circumstances, and we cheerfully shared our poor fare with him. . . .[16]

Three days later Delano met another lone traveller.

We fell in company this afternoon with a poor fellow who was working his way to California on foot, his sole supplies being a small bag of flour on his back. His cattle had died, and he had bought a horse. This, too, had died, and with a lame leg and a cancer on his hand, he was limping his way to that borne which was to salve all his aches and pains – the valley of the Sacramento.[16]

Not every company showed the humanity of Delano's. He tells of a harrowing case he heard of on 1 August on reaching the Humboldt River, where he found 'hundreds of wagons'. The victim was Joseph E. Ware, who had written and published a guidebook to California.

He was taken sick east of Fort Laramie, and his company, instead of affording him that protection which they were now more than ever bound to do, by the ties common to humanity, barbarously laid him by the road-side, without water, provisions, covering or medicines, to die! Suffering with thirst, he contrived to crawl off the road about a mile, to a pond, where he lay two days, exposed to a burning sun by day and cold winds by night, when Providence directed Fisher [*an acquaintance Delano had just met at the Humboldt*] and his mess to the same pond, where they found him. With a humanity which did them honor, they took him to their tent and nursed him two days; but nature, over-powered by exposure as well as disease, gave way, and he sank under his sufferings.[16]

In '49, as in earlier years, the most exhausting and punishing stretch of the trail for the emigrants was the forty miles of desert between the Humboldt Sink and Carson River. Beneath a relentless sun, oxen and wagon wheels sunk into alkali dust that rose in clouds to sting eyes and throat. For those late on the overland crossing there were alarming sights on this stretch of desert. One witness counted the bodies of 350 horses, 280 oxen, and 120 mules lying in dust. One thousand wagons had been abandoned, and with them beds, chests of drawers, and other furniture, as well as a wide assortment of household goods. And here and there crude markers indicated the shallow graves of men, women, and children who would never see the Promised Land of California.

The Royces were among the stragglers, and were fortunate to get through the desert without having to abandon their only wagon. Like the Donner Party of '46, the Royces took the route south of Great Salt Lake rather than the safer but slower trail via Fort Hall. They travelled by night to escape the fierce heat of day, but in doing so missed the turn off to the meadows where one could prepare animals, persons, and wagons for the difficult desert crossing. Instead, they entered upon the desert beyond the Humboldt Sink without pause for recruitment. With evidence at every mile of the disasters of other families, they pressed on grimly. One evening, Sarah Royce tells us, shortly before nightfall . . .

. . . as I had walked much of the afternoon, and knew I must walk again by and by, I was persuaded to get into the wagon and lie down by Mary, who was sleeping soundly. By a strong effort of will, backed by the soothing influence of prayer, I fell asleep, but only for a few minutes. I was roused by the stopping of the wagon, then my husband's voice said, 'So you've given out, have you Tom?' and at the same moment I knew by the rattling chains and yokes that some of the cattle were being loosed from the team. I was out of the wagon in a minute. One of the oxen was prostrate on the ground, and his companion, from whose neck the yoke was just being removed, looked very likely soon to follow him. It had been the weak couple all along. Now we had but two yoke. How soon would they, one by one, follow?

Nothing could induce me to get into the wagon again. I said I would walk by the team, and for awhile I did; but by and by I found myself yards ahead. An inward power urged me forward; and the poor cattle were so slow, it seemed every minute as if they were going to stop. When I got so far off as to miss the sound of foot-steps and wheels, I would pause, startled, wait and listen, dreading lest they had stopped, then as they came near, I would again walk beside them awhile, watching, through the darkness, the dim outlines of their heads and horns to see if they drooped lower. But soon I found myself again forward and alone. There was no moon yet, but by starlight we had for some time seen, only too plainly, the dead bodies of cattle lying here and there on both sides of the road. As we advanced they increased in numbers, and presently we saw two or three wagons. At first we thought we had overtaken a company, but coming close, no sign of life appeared. We had candles with us, and so, as there was not the least breeze, we lit one or two and examined. Everything indicated a complete break down, and a hasty flight. Some animals were lying nearly in front of a wagon, apparently just as they had dropped down, while loose yokes and chains indicated that part of the teams had been driven on, laden probably with some necessaries of life; for the contents of the wagons were scattered in confusion, the most essential articles alone evidently having been thought worth carrying. 'Ah,' we said, 'some belated little company has been obliged to pack what they could, and hurry to the river. Maybe it was the little company we met the other day.' It was not a very encouraging scene but our four oxen still kept their feet; we would drive on a little farther, out of this scene of ruin, bait them, rest ourselves and go on. We did so, but soon found that what we had supposed an exceptional misfortune must have been the common fate of many companies; for at still shortening intervals, scenes of ruin similar to that just described kept recurring till we seemed to be but the last, little, feeble, struggling band at the rear of a routed army.[39]

With so many white men on the trail, the Indians became more than ordinarily aggressive along the Humboldt. Delano says:

Scarcely a night passed without their making a raid upon some camp, and for five hundred miles they were excessively troublesome. If they could not drive the animals off, they would creep up behind the sage bushes in the night and shoot arrows into them, so that the animals would have to be left, when they would take them after the trains had passed. During the night it became a common practice for those on duty to discharge their firearms frequently, to show the Digger banditti that they were on the alert, but this precaution was not always effectual, and as we advanced, the tribes became more bold. They cannot be seen in the daytime, but at night they prowl about like vicious beasts, and pounce upon their prey with comparative safety.[16]

When his company halted at noon on 26 August eight miles from the pass through the Sierras, Delano made a hunting excursion to the mountains with two young men from a Missouri train.

I had preceded my companions along the border of a deep ravine, and was about fifty rods in advance, when the ravine terminated in a perpendicular wall of rock, hundreds of feet high, around which there appeared to be a craggy opening, or passage. While I was gazing on the towering rock before me, I momentarily changed my position, when the front part of my coat was grazed by something passing like a flash before me. Glancing at the base of the rock, I saw two naked Indians spring around a jutting, and I comprehended the matter at once. I had been a mark, and they had sent an arrow, which grazed my coat, but without striking me. I instantly raised my rifle and discharged it at the flying Indians, and sprang behind a tree. The noise of my piece soon brought my companions to my side, and going cautiously to the rock, a few stains of blood showed that my aim had not been decidedly bad; but we saw nothing more of the Indians.[16]

On 4 September, 250 miles from the mines and at least 200 from the nearest settlement, Delano met some horsemen, who gave an account of a fierce combat that had occurred a few days before between a small party of whites and some Indians.

The latter had become very bold and troublesome, not only on the Humboldt, but on the plains, and in the mountains this side. On the Humboldt they had made a foray, and driven off all the cattle belonging to a man who had a family with him. A call for volunteers was made, and a party at once formed to pursue the robbers. After tracing them some miles in the mountains, they found five head, which had been slaughtered, and the meat all picked from their bones. Here the party separated, and four men, two of the name of King, a Mr. Moore, and Mr. Elliot, taking a direction by themselves, while the others proceeded another way. Captain King, with whom I became well acquainted subsequently in the mines, corroborated the statement. His party had not gone far, when, on turning around a rock, they came in contact with four Indians, who drew their bows at once. Each man selected his antagonist, and a desperate fight for life commenced.

Elliot wounded his man mortally, though he commenced a flight. Moore had also wounded his, but he still continued to discharge his arrows before Moore could reload, who, to avoid the arrows, bent his head, but was severely wounded; while King, after wounding his, advanced, and after a desperate conflict dispatched him with his knife, after firing his pistol. The cap on Captain King's rifle exploded without discharging his gun, and his adversary discharged his arrows with great rapidity, without giving the Captain time to put on another cap. He however managed to dodge in time to avoid the arrows, and rushing up, caught hold of the Indian's bow with one hand, while the Indian seized the Captain's rifle. Thus they struggled until, becoming somewhat exhausted, they paused a moment, when King kicked his gun from the grasp of the Indian, and sprang after it. He avoided a second arrow, but as he was adjusting the cap, another arrow grazed his hand, inflicting a slight wound. His turn now came; the rifle was discharged, and the deadly weapon did its duty – the Indian fell dead. Elliot, being released by the death of his antagonist, rushed up to assist Moore, (who, though badly wounded, was still fighting desperately,) and shot the Indian with his pistol. Finding the odds now too great against him, the savage turned to retreat, but Elliot followed him with his knife, and inflicted a ghastly wound in his neck. Wounded as he was, the Indian now turned upon Elliot, who, with a pass of his knife, inflicted a wound in the Indian's abdomen, through which his bowels protruded, when he slowly sank to the ground, striking wildly, and with savage determination, at Elliot, with his own knife, and finally fell backwards in the agonies of death. . . .[16]

Delano reached what he felt to be the outposts of civilization on 17 September. His first sight of the Sacramento Valley brought joy.

Ascending to the top of an inclined plain, the long-sought, the long-wished-for and welcome valley of the Sacramento, lay before me, five or six miles distant.

How my heart bounded at the view! how every nerve thrilled at the sight! It looked like a grateful haven to the tempest-tossed mariner, and with long strides, regardless of the weariness of my limbs, I plodded on, anxious to set foot upon level ground beyond the barren, mountain desert. I could discern green trees, which marked the course of the great river, and a broad, level valley, but the day was too smoky for a very extended view. There was the resting place, at least for a few days, where the dangerous and weary nightwatch was no longer needed; where the habitations of civilized men existed, a security from the stealthy tread of the treacherous savage; where our debilitated frames could be renewed, and where our wandering would cease. . . . onward I pressed, till I reached the first trees which I had seen from the mountains, and found that they grew along the margin of Deer Creek, which I followed a mile, when the sight of a chimney attracted my attention. It was the house of Colonel Davis, eight miles from the foot hills.[16]

Delano was stricken with sudden self-consciousness on approaching the house :

Although it was a simple abode, standing within a rough paling, it was the first peaceful dwelling of civilized man which I had seen for months. While I hurried to it, I felt an almost irresistible repugnance to approach, and when at length I sat down in the porch, I felt lost and bewildered with a degree of astonishment at seeing men and women moving about at their usual avocations. I could only give short replies to interrogatories which were made, and after sitting nearly an hour in a kind of half stupidity, I found resolution enough to inquire where the trains were encamped.

'About a mile below', was the reply, and I got up and walked off,

leaving, probably, no very favorable impression as to my con-
versational powers.[16]

The Royces had set out from a village in Iowa in April. On 24 October
they reached what their guide-book called 'Pleasant Valley Gold
Mines' . . .

. . . where we found two or three tents, and a few men with their
gold-washing pans. They had been at work there for awhile; but said
the little 'diggings' just there were pretty much 'worked out'; and
they were going, in a day or two, over to Weaver Creek, where, they
told us, very fine 'prospects had lately been struck', and there was
quite a town growing up. That night, we slept, for the first time in
several months, without the fear of Indians, or the dread of perils
in advance. We rested ourselves and animals for two or three days,
and then moved into the village of 'Weaverville', of which the miners
had told us. This village was made up of tents, many of them very
irregularly placed; though in one part, following the trend of the
principal ravine, there was, already, something like a row of these
primitive dwellings, though at considerable distances apart. We
added one to that row, and soon began to gather about us little com-
forts and conveniences, which made us feel as though we once
more had a home. In a few days after we arrived in Weaverville,
rain fell heavily, and soon the mountains just above us were
blocked by snow. Only one company came through after us; and they
barely escaped, by means of good mules.[39]

Some families behind the Royces were caught in snowstorms on the
mountains, and might have perished but for successful relief missions.
Delano had this to say about the stragglers:

Those who started from the Missouri late in the season, or who,
by the vicissitudes of the plains, could not arrive till November,
experienced almost incredible hardships. The previous trains had
consumed all the grass, and thousands of cattle perished by the way.
The roads were lined with deserted wagons, and a vast amount of
other property; the Indians grew still more bold and troublesome
by success; and many families were reduced to the utmost distress,
with no means of getting forward but to walk. Provisions, which had
been abundant at the commencement of the journey, had been

thrown away, or abandoned with the wagons, and the last part of the emigration resembled the rout of an army, with its distressed multitudes of helpless sufferers, rather than the voluntary movement of a free people. Worn out with fatigue, and weak for want of nourishment, they arrived late in the season in the mountainous region of the Sierra Nevada, where still greater struggles stared them in the face. The rains and snow commenced much earlier than usual, and fell to an unprecedented depth; and it seemed utterly impossible for them to get through. In addition to other calamities, many suffered from scurvy and fevers – the consequence of using so much salt or impure provisions; and while many died, others were made cripples for life.

Reports of these sufferings reached the settlements, when the government, and individuals, who contributed largely, sent out a detachment to afford all the relief they could, and to bring the suffering emigrants in. The last of the emigrants had reached Feather River, on the Lawson route, when the government train reached them with mules. Some had been without food for two or three days, and with others a heavy body of snow lay on the ground. Three men made a desperate effort to get through. For some days they had been on an allowance of but one meal a day, when, packing up all the bread they had left, which was only a supply for two days, they started for Lawson's, a distance of seventy miles. The snow was between two and three feet deep, yet they waded through it for a few miles, when they came to a wagon containing two women and two or three children, who had eaten nothing for two or three days. With a generosity which was rare, under such circumstances, they gave all they had left to these helpless ones, and went on without. They succeeded in reaching Lawson's. Many knocked their exhausted cattle in the head, and lived upon them until the government train reached them. Women were seen wading through the deep snow, carrying their helpless children; and strong men dropped down from utter exhaustion. The only food they had was their animals, and men became so famished that they cut meat from the mules and horses which had perished from hunger and thirst by the road side. When the government train arrived, the women and children were placed upon the mules, exposed to a furious snow storm, in which many of the animals perished; but the emigrants finally succeeded in getting through, when the government furnished boats to carry them to Sacramento, as the roads along the valley had become impassable.[16]

But, as Delano points out, the emigrants on the California Trail in '49 were fortunate in one respect:

In 1849 there was more grass than had ever been known before. Traders who had been in the country fifteen or twenty years, assured us that they had never known such a plentiful season, and that grass was then growing in abundance where they never saw any before, and they universally said that had not such been the case it would have been utterly impossible for such an emigration to get through.[16]

People from many parts of the world were coming to California. There were direct sailings from European ports. Even Chinese came; many to open or work in laundries or restaurants in San Francisco. Mining made fortunes for a few men. Shrewdness enabled John Bidwell, trail pioneer of 1841, to make rich strikes, and he became one of California's wealthiest landowners. But after a few years rich finds became rare, and gold mining died out, leaving the mining towns deserted. Some of the miners went prospecting elsewhere, principally in Colorado, Nevada, Montana, and the Yukon; but most settled down to more humdrum occupations in California.

Certainly, California itself grew and prospered. The effect of the gold rush on California's growth in population and wealth was dramatic and lasting. By the boom year of 1852, when gold worth eighty-one million dollars was mined from Californian earth, the population had risen to a quarter of a million people, and by 1860 it had increased further to 380,000 people. This figure for 1860 can be contrasted with the populations in the same year for Oregon and Utah, 52,000 and 40,000 respectively. Yet by 1860 only 82,572 men in California were listed as miners.

The Mormons who had settled in the valley of the Great Salt Lake also prospered – just reward for their faith and courage in settling an area that others looked on only as inhospitable land to be crossed.

But settlement in the great region between the eastern frontier and the Pacific west was slow, until speeded up after the opening of the transcontinental railroad in 1869. The in-between years saw the Oregon and California trails become deeply rutted from the wheels of a busy flow of wagons. There was, too, the transitional transportation of the stagecoach. The Butterfield Overland Mail opened their stagecoach service on 16 September 1858, and made the overland crossing to California in less than four weeks. Then in 1862 Congress passed the Pacific Railroad Act, whereby two companies were authorized to link east and west of the American continent. The Civil War was then in progress, and President Lincoln considered that the building of the railroad would preclude any idea of California joining the Confederacy. On 10 May 1869 the rails from Sacramento in the west and from Omaha in the east were joined at Promontory Point, in Utah Territory. When the railroads sold land granted to them by the government – advertising both in America and in Europe, and running special trains for settlers – the frontier began to fade away. The transcontinental railroad ended, too, the era of the covered wagon. Fittingly, the steel tracks responsible for the wagon trains' demise followed closely the old trail opened up by the emigrants of the eighteen-forties.

Sources

1   Applegate, Jesse, *A Day with the Cow Column* (Transactions of the Oregon Pioneer Association), 1876; reprinted in *Oregon Historical Society Quarterly*, December 1900. Rucker, Maude Applegate (ed.), *The Oregon Trail and Some of its Blazers*, New York, 1930; Caxton Club, Chicago, Ill., 1934; the Champoeg Press, Portland, Oregon, 1952.

2   Applegate, Jesse A., *Recollections of My Boyhood*, Roseburg, Oregon, 1914; reprinted in Rucker, Maude Applegate (ed.), *The Oregon Trail and Some of its Blazers*, New York, 1930.

3   Atherton, Mr., The Washington *Globe*, 13 March 1849.

4   Bidwell, John, *A Journey to California*, San Francisco, Cal., 1937; a reprint of a booklet in the Bancroft Library, University of California.

5   Bidwell, John, *Echoes of the Past about California*, ed. Milo Milton Quaife, Chicago, Ill., 1928; serialized in *The Century Magazine*, 1890/91, and published as a pamphlet by the Chico *Advertiser*, about 1914.

6   Breen, John: Farnham, Eliza W., *California, in-doors and out; or, how we farm, mine and live generally in the golden state*, New York, 1856.

7   Breen, Patrick: *Diary of Patrick Breen, one of the Donner party*, ed. Frederick J. Taggart, Berkeley, Cal., 1910 (Pub.ications of the Academy of Pacific Coast History, vol. 1, no. 6); reprinted in George Rippey Stewart, *Ordeal by Hunger: The Story of the Donner Party*, Berkeley, Cal., 1936; new ed., New York, 1960; London, 1962. The original manuscript of Breen's Diary is in the Bancroft Library, University of California.

8   Bruff, J. Goldsborough: Read, Georgia Willis & Gaines, Ruth (eds), *Gold Rush: The Journals, Drawings and other Papers of J. Goldsborough Bruff*, 2 vols, New York, 1944.

9   Bryant, Edwin, *What I saw in California: being the Journal of a Tour, by the Emigrant Route and South Pass of the Rocky Mountains, across the Continent of North America, the Great Desert Basin, and through California, in the Years 1846, 1847*, New York, 1848.

10 Burnett, Peter Hardeman, *Recollections and Opinions of an Old Pioneer*, New York, 1880.

11 The *California Star*, San Francisco, Cal., 13 February 1847.

12 Chenoweth, The Hon. F. A., An Address in Transactions of the Oregon Pioneer Association, 1882; quoted by Ghent, William James, *The Road to Oregon: A Chronicle of the Great Emigrant Trail*, New York, 1929.

13 Clayton, William, *Journal: A Daily Record of the Journey of the Original Company of 'Mormon' Pioneers from Nauvoo, Illinois, to the Valley of the Great Salt Lake*, Salt Lake City, Utah, 1921.

14 Clyman, James: Camp, Charles L. (ed.), *James Clyman, American Frontiersman, 1792-1881: the adventures of a trapper and covered wagon emigrant as told in his own reminiscences and diaries*, San Francisco, Cal., 1928 (California Historical Society, Special Publication No. 3).

15 Colton, Rev. Walter, U.S.N., *Three Years in California*, New York, 1850; reprinted Stanford, Cal., 1949.

16 Delano, Alonzo, *Life on the Plains and among the Diggings; being Scenes and Adventures of an Overland Journey to California*, New York, 1857.

17 De Smet, Pierre Jean, S. J., *Letters and Sketches* (1843); reprinted in Thwaites, Reuben Gold, LL.D. (ed.), *Early Western Travels 1748-1846*, vol. xxvii, Cleveland, Ohio, 1906, part 2.

18 Field, Matthew C.: Gregg, Kate L. & McDermott, J. F. (eds), *Prairie and Mountain Sketches*, Norman, Oklahoma, 1957 (American Exploration and Travel Series, vol. 29).

19 Frémont, John Charles, *Narrative of the Exploring Expedition to the Rocky Mountains, In the Year 1842, and to Oregon and North California, In the years 1843-44*, London, 1846; reprinted in Nevins, Allan (ed.), *Narratives of Exploration and Adventure*, New York, 1956.

20 Graves, Mary Ann: quoted by McGlashan, Charles Fayette, *History of the Donner Party: A Tragedy of the Sierra*, Truckee, Cal. 1879.

21 Hastings, Lansford Warren, *The Emigrants' Guide to Oregon and California*, Cincinnati, Ohio, 1845; reprinted Princeton, N.J. 1932 (Narratives of the Trans-Mississippi Frontier).

22 Houghton, Eliza P. Donner, *The Expedition of the Donner Party and its Tragic Fate*, Chicago, Ill., 1911.

23 Johnson, Overton & Winter, Wm. H., *Route across the Rocky Mountains*, Lafayette, Indiana, 1846; reprinted in *Oregon Historical Society Quarterly*, March 1906, and Princeton, N.J., 1932 (Narratives of the Trans-Mississippi Frontier).

24 Kane, Thomas Leiper: Winther, O. O. (ed.), *A Friend of the Mormons*, San Francisco, Cal., 1937.

25 Kelly, William, J. P., *An Excursion to California over the Prairie, Rocky Mountains, and Great Sierra Nevada*, 2 vols, London, 1851.

26 Keseberg, Lewis: quoted by McGlashan, Charles Fayette, *History of the Donner Party: A Tragedy of the Sierra*, Truckee, Cal., 1879.

27 Mackay, Charles, *The Mormons: or Latter-Day Saints, with memoirs of the life and death of Joseph Smith, the 'American Mahomet'*, London, 1851.

28 Marsh, John: letter published in the *Daily Argus*, St Louis, Missouri, 31 October 1840.

29 Marsh, John: Lyman, George D., *John Marsh, Pioneer: The Life Story of a Trail-blazer on Six Frontiers*, New York, 1930.

30 Marshall James: interview printed in *Hutchings' California Magazine*, November 1857; reproduced in facsimile by Hawgood, John A., *The American West*, London, 1967 (published in the U.S.A. as *America's Western Frontiers*).

31 Mason, Colonel R. B.: in appendix to Frémont, John Charles, *Geographical Memoir upon Upper California in Illustration of his Map of Oregon and California*, Washington, 1848; reprinted in San Francisco, Cal., 1964.

32 Memorial by citizens of the Territory of California to the Governor, R. F. Stockton, January 1847; quoted by McGlashan, Charles Fayette, *History of the Donner Party: A Tragedy of the Sierra*, Truckee, Cal., 1879.

33 *The Millennial Star*, 1 February 1848; quoted by Linn, William Alexander, *The Story of the Mormons: from the date of their Origin to the Year 1901*, New York, 1902.

34 Nesmith, James W., 'Diary of the Emigration of 1843', in *Oregon Historical Society Quarterly*, December 1906.

35 Painsville, Ohio, *Telegraph*, 24 May 1843; quoted by Drury, Clifford Merrill, Ph.D., *Marcus Whitman, M.D.: Pioneer and Martyr*, Caldwell, Idaho, 1937.

36 Parkman, Francis, Jr, *The California and Oregon Trail: being Sketches of Prairie and Rocky Mountain Life*, New York, 1849; and various editions.

37 Polk, James Knox: in appendix to Frémont, John Charles, *Geographical Memoir upon Upper California in Illustration of his Map of Oregon and California*, Washington, 1848; reprinted in San Francisco, Cal., 1964.

38 Reed, Virginia: letter dated 16 May 1847, quoted by George Rippey Stewart, *Ordeal by Hunger: The Story of the Donner Party*, Berkeley, Cal., 1936; new ed., New York, 1960; London, 1962.

39 Royce, Sarah Eleanor: Gabriel, Ralph Henry (ed.), *A Frontier Lady: Recollections of the Gold Rush and early California*, New Haven, Conn., 1932.

40 Snow, Erastus, *Discourse on the Utah Pioneers*, Salt Lake City, Utah, 1880.

41 Sutter, John Augustus: interview printed in *Hutchings' California Magazine*, November 1857; reproduced in facsimile by Hawgood, John A., *The American West*, London, 1967

42 Talbot, Captain Theodore: Carey, Charles H. (ed.), *The Journals of Theodore Talbot 1843 and 1849-52*, Portland, Oregon, 1931.

43 Thornton, Jessy Quinn, *Oregon and California in 1848*, 2 vols, New York, 1849.

44 Whitman, Marcus: Drury, Clifford Merrill, Ph.D., *Marcus Whitman, M.D.: Pioneer and Martyr*, Caldwell, Idaho, 1937.

45 Williams, Joseph, *Narrative of a tour from the State of Indiana to the Territory in the Years 1841-2* (privately printed), Cincinnati, Ohio, 1843; reprinted in a limited edition, Cadmus Book Shop, New York, 1921; further reprinted in Hafen, LeRoy R. & Ann W. (eds), *To the Rockies and Oregon 1839-1842*, Glendale, Cal., 1955.

Index